COLLECTING
ORIGINAL PRINTS

27/95. "Penne—Aveyron"   Cedric Green viii95

COLLECTING ORIGINAL PRINTS

Rosemary Simmons HON RE

A & C BLACK

LONDON

First published in Great Britain in 2005
A & C Black Publishers Limited
Alderman House
37 Soho Square
London W1D 3QZ
www.acblack.com

ISBN-10: 0-7136-6847-4
ISBN-13: 978-0-7136-6847-6
Copyright © 2005 Rosemary Simmons HonRE

CIP Catalogue records for this book are available from the British Library and the U.S. Library of Congress.

Book design by Jo Tapper
Cover design by Sutchinda Rangsi Thompson
Copyedited by Julian Beecroft
Project Manager: Susan Kelly

Printed in Singapore by Star Standard

A & C Black uses paper produced with elemental chlorine-free pulp, harvested from managed sustainable forests.

Frontispiece:
Penne, Aveyron by Cedric Green, 1994. Hard-ground etching on zinc with added fractinted texture (see p115), 330 x 330 mm (13 x 13 in). Printed and published by the artist in an edition of 75.

CONTENTS

ACKNOWLEDGEMENTS

I would like to thank all the artists who have contributed their own prints to help illustrate this book. Many print galleries and publishers have been generous in loaning images; museums and private collections have also been very helpful. Thanks to Jane Stobart RE for the diagrams explaining the printing techniques.

I particularly want to thank members of the Royal Society of Painter-Printmakers, with whom I have been discussing the knotty problem of defining what makes an original print. They and all other independent printmakers are affected by the lack of general knowledge of the subject outside their own profession, particularly the confusion between artists' original prints and reproductions. We have reached a working formula, explored in the first part of this book; it relies, however, on the interested public making the effort to understand what motivates an artist to take the arduous route of making an artist's original print rather than the easy way of replicating an existing image through commercial printing. Some artists will not agree to this definition, and those publishers and galleries who make money from reproductions will not accept it, but others will welcome the clarification, perhaps becoming excited by understanding and then collecting artists' original prints.

Seven Figures Waiting by Bartolomeu dos Santos RE, 1988. Photo-etching and aquatint, 570 x 600 mm (22⅜ x 23⅝ in.). Printed and published by the artist in an edition of 30.

FOREWORD

Peakland: Winter Apple by Rosemary Simmons HonRE, 1966. Relief print, 430 x 580 mm (17 x 22¾ in). Published by the artist in an edition of 25. The artist says, 'The background block was plywood, and printed in two yellow water-based inks blended in the Japanese *bokashi* method. Three lino blocks formed the top and sides using oil-based inks. The tree was first drawn in Indian ink and then sent to a process engraver's where a photo-etched zinc line block of the image was made, which was then printed in black oil-based ink. The tree shadows were printed from lino in transparent brown oil-based ink and the yellow apples touched in by brush. The edition was printed on an 1868 Albion press.'

I have to admit that I have been obsessed with printing since I saw *The Times* being printed in London on a school visit. When I started my art training I was introduced to printmaking and realised that artists can use print too as part of their work. Since those early days I have, by luck or design, made prints in most printmaking media, run a print gallery and an artists' lithographic studio, taught in art colleges, lectured to both specialist and non-specialist groups, written a number of books about printmaking and started an international magazine on printmaking; and still, I have to say, I find it the most fascinating art form.

For technical and cultural reasons it is always developing. In times of war or economic recession artists have made prints with the most meagre of materials: floorboards, ink made from soot and grease and printed on scrap paper by hand. In times of affluence artists have access to expensive technology and the assistance of master printers, and thus they can make the most extravagant creations possible. In each case the creative work will reflect the time and place in which it was made, and thus the print becomes an historical document as well as a work of art. In fact, the more dramatic and humanly touching work is often done when times are difficult for the artist. The ingenuity of artists is a striking facet of the development of printmaking, one which constantly amazes and delights me.

I hope this book conveys my love of printmaking and perhaps opens a door for the reader on what may have seemed a puzzling world.

SECTION ONE

Run for your Country, Run for your Life by Simon Brett RE, 2003. Wood engraving, 202 x 251 mm (8 x 9⅞ in.). Part of 'The Axe of God' series, printed and published by the artist in an edition of 60.

The artist says, *'This is part of an ongoing series. Being quite large they are not typical of wood engraving in this country [UK]. When the series is complete, perhaps at 12 prints, part of the edition will be presented as a boxed set.'*

Introduction to Collecting

Collecting is a universal activity. Art objects have always been high on the list of collectables because they offer such a wide range of scale and value. This book offers guidance to anyone interested in collecting artists' original prints made since 1900; it defines what they are and explains how they can be recognised; it relates how printmaking developed as an artist's medium; and it sets out the various kinds of prints made today and tells you where you can see them.

Many people start by randomly buying or being given a few pictures and gradually finding that they like one kind instead of another; their growing passion may eventually boil down to a particular subject matter or technique and a desire to know more about it. Whilst it is true that many people buy works of art or furniture or ceramics on the basis of 'Does it appeal to me?', that is not real collecting. The collector wants to know who made it, how, when, who it has been owned by before and how it fits into the history of art. Perhaps some people will also want to know if it is being offered at a reasonable price and has potential resale value in the future.

Collecting artists' original prints is popular because all depths of purse or bank account can be satisfied. Buying just one small print a year can eventually result in a really fine collection if you choose wisely. Of course,

Opposite:
Big Beats by Anthony Frost, 1999. Screenprint with wood block, 1130 x 760mm (44½ x 30 in.). Printed and published by Advanced Graphics London in an edition of 75.

to build a spectacular collection of world-museum class you would, today, need to spend a very large sum indeed; but, unlike some forms of collecting – furniture or pre-20th century painting, for example – you can start to collect artist's prints at any level.

Most artists prefer to think that the key emotion aroused in anyone buying their work is one of pleasure: understanding what the artist is trying to communicate and enjoying the way they have realised that message. Art is a non-verbal language and like any language it pays to understand it better. Artists rarely go out of their way to create something merely for its preciousness; they want to communicate their own excitement or pleasure in the subject matter. This could be anything from a small black-and-white wood engraving of a mouse to the intellectual idea behind an abstract screenprint in sumptuous colour. Every work of art needs both creator and observer in order to exist. If you collect for pleasure the works you buy will reward you with years of visual enjoyment and mental stimulation. If your tastes and interests change over the years, your collection of prints will reflect this change; early enthusiasms may be relegated to the bathroom or loft, only to reappear again years later when fashions change and another generation has started to seek them out.

Some people collect for investment, either thinking about a nest egg for their old age or possibly a much shorter speculation aimed at selling within a few years. The former is an easier project to carry through, as long as you can build and keep a collection for some 40–50 years, during which period the artists you initially bought will have gone through the seemingly natural process of success, neglect and reappraisal which characterises the art market.

Speculative collecting over a shorter timescale is not for the faint-hearted, and you'll need some luck to spot a cultural trend at its beginning and to sell at the height of its fashionability, before it is replaced by the next trend. There has always been an element of fashion in art, and today it is exploited very widely by the media, especially if scandal or sensation can be attached to either work or artist. A recent survey by the website artprice.com said that 'lower-priced prints and lithographs have rewarded investors. Portfolios of prints bought for less than 1,000 euros have shown annual gains of 16.5 per cent since 1996'. The typical source for trendsetting art is to be found at the art college end-of-year diploma or graduation exhibitions. It is worth going to several of these shows, which are usually within a few weeks of each other at the end of the academic year, and are invariably advertised in art magazines. Those collectors who have early works from innovators find that these pieces will always be valuable as historical documents at the very least. This kind of speculation, though, tends to turn collecting into a cold-blooded business, and is not suited to many temperaments.

Prints for public and domestic spaces

An important motivation for collecting in the last 50 years has been to improve a workplace space, not with any future value in mind but to

Pineapple by Barbara Jones, 1971. Lithograph, 775 x 613 mm (30 x 22 in.), printed and published by Curwen Prints Ltd in an edition of 100.
This was one of a series of eight *Follies* and shows a fantastical building at Dunmore Park in Stirlingshire, Scotland. The artist was a lifelong recorder of quirky British architecture and artefacts. The image was drawn by the artist on zinc plate.

humanise the space or create a certain ambience for the people working there. Many large companies have considerable corporate collections of artists' original prints in their offices, corridors and canteens, lending large spaces a more human scale. The British Government has a fine collection of works of art including prints for embassies, the Civil Service and government offices. Not only does it support artists and provide a showcase for talent, it also gives the temporary owner some control over their working environment.

Hospitals and similar institutions often have quite extensive collections of artists' prints, which, when framed in unbreakable 'glass', are an inexpensive way of providing distraction, hope or solace in a stressful atmosphere. Subjects chosen tend to be somewhat bland and inoffensive,

Red Assembly by Brian Rice, 1964. Screenprint, 737 × 737 mm (29 × 29 in.). Printed and published by the artist. The artist says that his work of this period *'was strongly influenced by De Stijl and European Constructivist art of the 1920s and 1930s'.*

but they do not have to be just pretty landscapes, and will probably be more successful if they are intriguing, witty or they tell a story.

Many public libraries used to have loan collections of prints, though these seem to have disappeared in recent years. Print clubs were common in Scandinavia, particularly in banks and other large organisations, where employees would take turns in spending an annual budget on works of art for the offices or to borrow prints for their own homes. This practice also seems to have gone as businesses have become anonymously internationalised. Schools once made a habit of buying real works of art rather than the ubiquitous reproduction; few have the funds these days.

Most artist's prints are hung in individual homes, for which, in terms of scale and intimacy, they are peculiarly well suited.

The art market

The art market can be as unstable as any other, and realising an investment is a matter of good timing. If in making a collection you have half an eye on the future value of what you are buying, it is worth considering the following guidelines to help mitigate the risk.

Grouping your collection by subject matter is an obvious choice. A group of prints of a local landscape/townscape will always find a market if your chosen area has some heritage or other tourist attraction. Likewise, specialist collections of animals, classic cars, architecture, concrete poetry, artist-designed wine labels, bookplates – the list is endless, but each will have its own band of enthusiasts.

Another rewarding way of collecting is by technique: mezzotint and copper engraving are not very widely practised, being slow to accomplish and requiring a great deal of skill. Both fell out of favour a long time ago, and, though mezzotint has been revived in recent years, engraving on metal is still rare: young artists will not spend the time to learn the skill; they want quicker results. Some collectors specialise in stone lithography; others favour wood engravings of the 1920s and '30s.

Some collectors will only buy an artist's proof (the part of the edition that the artist keeps for their own archive) or else print number one from an edition. Others look out for a print dedicated by the artist to a friend, thereby having two interesting characters – artist and beneficiary – linked in the one piece. Some people will only buy a print from a very small edition, thinking it to be more precious; others celebrate the democracy of a larger edition. All these self-imposed restrictions will give the collection a special character and can make it easier to sell in the future at a specialised auction or fair.

Such attitudes to collecting are rather cold and calculating, though equally there are artists who use their skills to make works for a specifically defined market. This book will try, however, to suggest a form of collecting which appreciates the world of creative printmaking in all its variety.

What is an Artist's Original Print?

It would be convenient if there was a simple way of defining an artist's original print that was universally accepted. There is a great deal of confusion conjured up just by the word 'print'; it covers so many things, from newspapers, posters, even wallpapers, to reproductions of famous paintings, to original etchings and other artist-made prints. A reproduction of Constable's *Flatford Mill*, for example, is not an artist's original print, but an inadequate approximation of an oil painting that in the flesh is probably of quite a different size. If it is printed on canvas and has brushstrokes simulated in varnish (called an oleograph), it is more of a joke than a deception. A reproduction is a copy of a pre-existing work, which may be crudely printed with garish colours quite different from the original or else may be a facsimile (same size as the original) that perfectly reproduces every nuance, such as a museum facsimile of a manuscript that is too fragile to handle. Reproductions do have an important place as a teaching aid or as an aide-memoire of a favourite work. The reproductions of contemporary paintings that you see in abundance in framing shops to me seem like lifeless objects, and are very far from being original prints because they are so remote from the artists who created the original images.

The artist's signature

The signing of prints was rare until the late 19th century, though earlier artists such as Albrecht Dürer (1471–1528) did try to protect their copyright by incorporating a monogram within the design. Old prints usually had a series of terms in Latin (see Glossary) engraved under the image, which identified the artist who designed the print, the craftsman-engraver, the printer and the publisher – this was required by law to prevent sedition.

In Mid-Victorian England, a Royal Academician named Francis Seymour Haden (1818–1910) wanted to differentiate his own creative prints from the reproductive engravings after other artists' paintings, which the Academy routinely allowed to be exhibited, so he signed his own prints in pencil in a campaign to elevate the status of artists' prints. Furious at having his own etchings rejected by the Academy (on the grounds of being ineligible), in 1880 he founded the Society of Painter-Etchers, now known as The Royal Society of Painter-Printmakers. He also tried to find an acceptable definition of what we now call 'original prints', but there were many disagreements. One of these contentious areas concerned the camera, and whether it was in the same category as the pencil or the brush, whether it was just another tool for the artist to use, or whether a photographic print counted as an original creation.

Today, we tend to accept some photographs as genuinely creative, but treat such images differently from press photographs or family snaps.

Definitions

Many attempts have been made from 1960 onwards to craft a watertight definition of what constitutes an artist's original print, but all have failed for trying to limit the work by technique. Artists, being creative animals, will use whatever is available to them, so when a new material or method appears, usually in the commercial world first, they will invariably want to use it in ways that commerce never envisaged.

In 1960 the International Association of Plastic Arts, a UNESCO affiliate made up of artists, stated that an original print must be printed by the artist alone, must be signed and numbered in a limited edition, and that the printing matrix (the plates, blocks or stones) must be cancelled once the printing of the edition is complete.

This seems to have been the first use of the term 'original print'. 'Original' is used in the dictionary definition of the word, 'thinking or acting for oneself, inventive, creative, an original mind'. The idea in 1960 was to make a clear distinction between a print created entirely by an artist using the traditional printmaking techniques, and reproductions, using photomechanical commercial printing techniques, of pre-existing paintings. This definition was broadly accepted at the time by artists, art teachers, art societies, auctioneers and museums, but not wholeheartedly by art dealers, framing shops and some publishers of reproductions, who wanted the freedom to imply that their products were intrinsically as

valuable as original prints. These publishers started calling their reproductions 'limited editions' (usually rather large editions), getting the artist of the pre-existing painting to sign each reproduction. They called these images 'fine-art prints' and 'lithographs'. Printmakers were incensed that their terminology was being appropriated for products inherently different from their own creative use of traditional printing techniques that had been long since abandoned by commercial printing.

The matter was complicated, as each country adopted different criteria, but all were agreed that an original print should have no photographic elements whatsoever. This was happening in the early 1960s, just at the time when artists were becoming excited about new developments in technology, namely screenprinting, which allowed for the incorporation of photographic elements and the printing of large areas of intense opaque colours on many surfaces other than the traditional paper. Artists were never going to listen to the absurd restrictions placed on them by legislators, so the 1960 definitho fell by the wayside.

More recent attempts to find definitions based on techniques have also failed. Once artists had access to digital technology, naturally they wanted to use it as they had screenprinting 20 years earlier. Every new technique will be seized upon and experimented with by artists and will prove a

Euston by Rosura Jones (aka Rosemary Simmons HonRE), 1965. Offset lithograph, 460 x 610 mm (18 x 24 in). Printed and published by Curwen Prints Ltd in an unlimited edition, not signed or numbered.
The print commemorates the famous Euston Arch pulled down by municipal vandals when Euston Station, London, was modernised. The arch and the historical engraving parts were photocopied onto acetate film and the tall dark shapes simulating tall modern buildings were made by rolling black ink onto acetate; these were then used to make photolitho plates but without a halftone screen. The image is printed in five colours onto a machine-made cartridge paper.

challenge to museum curators and collectors and those who like neat boundaries. The *giclée*, or digital print, is the current problem: it can be printed on demand and is mostly used by reproduction publishers and by people making fakes of old prints, maps and drawings. The technology is so good (it is a superior digital form of colour copying) it is even used to copy works by 20th-century masters such as Pablo Picasso (1881–1973) and Henry Moore (1898–1986), and such reproductions are sometimes offered as originals to the unwary. At the same time some artists are using *giclée* to print their own truly exciting digitally created original prints. It is not easy for members of the public to make an informed choice: how do you know if what you are buying is an original print or a reproduction?

As with any form of collecting, it is important to understand the field. An original print will always have the direct presence of the artist speaking to you; its value is intrinsic and real. Reproductions have a very minor resale value, and auction houses of repute will not sell them.

Limited editions

The original reasons for limiting the size of an edition were twofold: some printing plates, such as those used in drypoint technique, quickly wear down, with the result that after a certain number the impressions will no longer be perfect; at the same time, it has always been important to the public and dealers that the work they buy is scarce, precious, or, as the artist Howard Hodgkin sees it, 'more personal'. Collectors also wanted to know that an image would not be repeated indefinitely, and so to guarantee rarity it used to be common for the artist to cancel the printing matrix in some way; this is rarely practised today.

Cannon Street Bridge by Joseph Winkelman PPRE, 2002. Etching from copper plate, 300 x 600 mm (11¾ x 23½ in). Printed and published by the artist in an edition of 100.

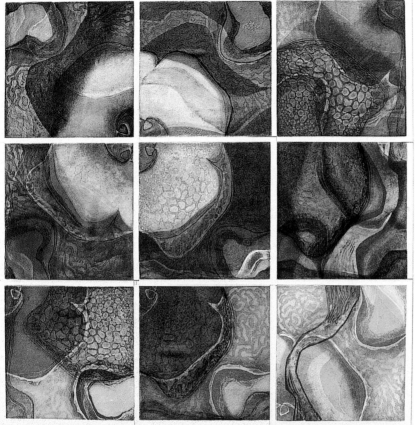

Fleurs Imaginaires by Cedric Green, 1997. Electrolytic etching on zinc, 600 x 600 mm (23 ⅝ x 23 ⅝ in). Printed and published by the artist.
The artist says, '*An edition is not applicable because the image is a unique collage of printed squares. The three plates are overprinted in intaglio and relief, turned to give a very large number of variations of effect and colours, and then chosen to make up collages, all different.*'

The problem from an artist's point of view is simply one of protecting their livelihood and preserving their skills. If a reproduction is available at a price similar to an original print it makes a mockery of all the creative work put into the original print: there is no appreciation of the skill, knowledge and time that the printmaker has invested in producing it. Many other craft-based skills, such as ceramics, draw a clear distinction these days between mass-produced plates and what are known as 'studio' pots. The same is true of craft textiles, glass, jewellery and silversmithing. All these disciplines, and printmaking too, hover uneasily over old separations between what is art and what is craft. Today, artists do not accept these divisions, and perhaps it is better to think of the end product as a work of fine art arrived at via craft-based skills.

Another definition

A recent attempt to clarify the confusion surrounding original prints grew out of an American idea to put the onus on the print publisher (which could mean anyone from the individual artist to a large company) to disclose how a print was made, by what means and by whom. The larger

American publishers gave a certificate of authentication including all these details with each editioned print, so that buyers could make up their own minds. Then the reproduction manufacturers did the same in imitation, though their information was often scanty, and evasive as to the true size of editions and the manufacturing process.

The classification of prints

In Britain in the 1980s, a committee was set up by the Fine Art Trade Guild (the trade association of reproduction printers, publishers and frame shops) to discuss the matter. The Royal Society of Painter-Printmakers, the Royal Academy and the Fine Print Dealers' Association were invited to send delegates. After many heated discussions an agreement was reached and adopted by the British Standards Institute and published in 1996 (BS 7876) as *The Classification of Prints*. In it, categories were assigned according to the extent of the artist's involvement in making each print. The agreement begins: 'This British Standard establishes a system of categories for all print production and distinguishes the print according to the extent to which the artist named as inventor was actually involved in making the print.'

BS 7876 did require the words 'reproduction' and 'facsimile' to be used wherever appropriate, and artists' prints were to be referred to by the actual process used in their making (aquatint, woodcut, etc.). The techniques used for artists' prints and those used for commercial reproductions are described later in this book, and short definitions can be found in the glossary.

This British Standard seemed to offer the public an easy way to recognise the differences between one sort of print and another, allowing them to exercise their own judgement in assessing the value of a print at the time they come to buy it and also its likely future worth.

Unfortunately, the British Standards Institute was selling the document for a high price and would not let it be quoted in full without payment. Furthermore, the agreement had no sanctions attached to it by law and was given no publicity, and it has since been forgotten. You will not find it being used in any gallery, museum or framing shop.

Degrees of involvement

The idea that an artist might have varying degrees of involvement in making a particular work of art is not new. In the past painters and sculptors often had apprentices to whom they taught their trade and who in return helped the master to make the finished work. These assistants ground colours, mixed varnish, stretched canvas and often painted parts of the background, leaving the master to do the detailed work. The intellectual idea behind the work was, of course, entirely that of the master not the apprentice. The same happened in the sculptor's workshop, where the pupils often made the armature for a modelled work or roughly shaped a stone for a carver. These assistants were employed to do the boring routine work involved in making any work of art.

The development of printmaking followed the same pattern, with printers employed to assist in the arduous work of printing: before motors were attached to printing presses, the work of applying enough pressure to lift the film of ink off the plate and onto the paper was hard physical labour. Gradually another sort of jobbing workshop evolved, run by printers for artists who did not have their own equipment. The situation could arise that, as printing itself became more sophisticated, an artist might not have enough experience to realise a work in the way he or she envisaged it; in this instance, the printer would offer guidance to the artist as to how to make a technically correct printing surface or matrix. If the relationship between artist and printer was really good, the end product could be excellent both technically and in its realisation of the artist's intentions; some of the most exciting late-20th-century artist's original prints are the result of a collaboration, even as others have been produced by the artist working entirely alone.

William Scott (left) with Stanley Jones, discussing a lithographic proof in the first Curwen Studio in London, 1960. The clothes pegs and line were used to hang up proofs to dry between colours.

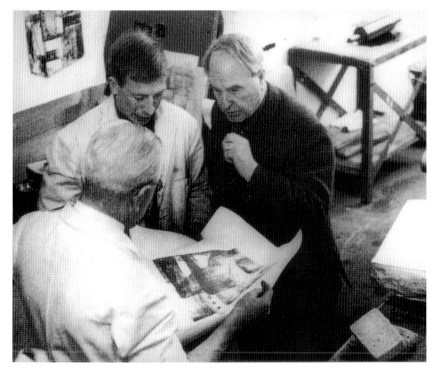

Henry Moore (right) is discussing a lithographic proof of *Square Forms* with Stanley Jones, master printer (centre) and another printer at the Curwen Studio in 1963. In the background can be seen the inking table and roller (top right) and lower down the corner of a lithographic stone and a dampening sponge. The lithograph was published by Galerie Wolfgang Ketterer, Stuttgart and Felix H. Mann, London, in the portfolio *Europaische Graphik VI* in 1968 in an edition of 100.

Of course, there are many degrees of collaboration, and in all fields of fine art today artists frequently buy in skills they do not have themselves: wanting to use a shark in formaldehyde in your installation does not mean you need to learn how to catch sharks. In many eyes artistic skills are no longer highly regarded; what really matters is the initial idea, not how or by whom it was made. Traditionally, creative people have earned a living by selling their work or licensing its copying in return for royalties. Now there is a strong movement which says all art, music and literature should be free over the Internet, and that the real contribution of the artist is the intellectual idea alone. Many printmakers do sell their work on the Internet, but they also find it being copied without payment, thus negating the purpose of limiting and signing each print.

The basic categories

An uneasy convention accepts that there are two distinct groups of prints.

Original prints

The artist creates the image using printmaking techniques. The image does not already exist in another medium and is not complete until the final colour is printed and the print is numbered and signed. This category may be subdivided into prints made entirely by the artist from beginning to end and those where there is a degree of collaboration with a technician.

Digital prints can be original prints if the image is wholly or largely made by the artist using a computer and the complete image did not already exist in another medium. Details of how the print was made and its edition status should be signed by the artist and be available on request to a buyer.

Eve by Charlotte Hodes, 2000. Tetronix wax ink-jet print, 380 x 250 mm (15 x 10 in). Printed and published by the artist in an edition of 30.

The artist says, *'This is one of a series of digital prints based on Durer's painting* Eve, *which is in the Prado, Madrid. A postcard of this painting and a section of wallpaper were scanned into the computer. They were manipulated through Photoshop using various dithering techniques. Numerous proofs were taken in order to refine the colour.'*

Reproductions

The artist has given a pre-existing painting or drawing to a commercial printer, who prepares it for printing either by photolithography or for digital ink-jet output. The artist has made no contribution to the print itself. Publishers may ask the artist to sign the print and it may be issued in an edition. If the artist makes use of photocopiers or scanning to create a work by collage and mixed media and then makes a colour copy of this pre-existing artwork, the copy remains a reproduction.

A Short History of Printmaking

The earliest form of printmaking is often claimed to be the hand impressions found on prehistoric cave walls; true printmaking, however, has its roots in China, where religious texts were carved on woodblocks and printed. The most significant invention to advance the art of printing was that of paper around 105AD. Also first made in China, it later spread to Japan and along the trade routes to the West, and was first made in Europe in Spain in 1115AD.

Woodblocks were probably first used in the West to print patterns on fabric. By the early 15th century they were also widely used in the making of block books, complete pages of text and illustrations carved from a single piece of wood, as well as for thousands of individual prints of religious pictures, indulgences, popular tales and playing cards sold at fairs and shrines. But important books were still handwritten by scribes in monasteries, and, though the demand for them was great, the printing of block books was almost as slow as handwriting. How widely known in the West was the Korean invention of movable type is uncertain. However, Johann Gutenberg (1397–1468) in Mainz, Germany, brought together the skills of engraving and casting metal (he was a goldsmith) with a refinement of the wooden screw press and an improved ink. By 1450 he was able to print his famous 42-line Bible with movable metal type. This breakthrough in producing text relatively easily and cheaply aided the spread of literacy, and by 1480 there were printing presses throughout Christian Europe.

In illustrated and decorated books the metal type was printed first and the embellished initials and pictures printed later from woodcuts. The grain of wood restricts the fineness of detail that can be cut, and illustrators soon turned to the ancient techniques of engraving metal and etching it in acid. These highly developed skills were used to decorate armour, weapons and both domestic and church plate. Indeed, goldsmiths and silversmiths sold patterns for copying in the form of prints taken by rubbing ink into the lines incised on the metal and then pressing it onto paper. It was a short step to making illustrations for books in the same way; though requiring different ink and different amounts of pressure, they still had to be printed separately from the type.

Illustration becomes art

Early Western prints, generally by anonymous artists, were used to illustrate books that were deemed to be of great value; single prints were just items of ephemera and rarely survive. It was only in the early 16th century that printmaking became an independent art form, when artists of the stature of Dürer recognised it as a versatile medium that would enable him to spread his work far and wide. As an apprentice, Dürer had worked as one of the many artisans who produced over 600 woodcuts to illustrate the *Nuremberg Chronicle of the World* of 1493. From 1498 Dürer worked as an independent master, producing a number of impressive woodcuts, but he

Nach Christus gepurt.1513. Jar.Adi.j.May. Hat man dem grosmechtigen Kunig von Portugall Em anuell gen Lysabona pracht auß India/ein sollich lebendig Thier. Das nennen sie Rhinocerus.Das ist hye mit aller seiner gestalt Absondertset.Es hat ein farb wie ein gesprecklete Schildkro t.Vnd ist võ dicken Schalen vberlegt fast fest.Vnd ist in der gröf als der Helfandt Aber nydertrechtiger von paynen/vnd fast werhafftig.Es hat ein scharff starck Horn vorn auff der nasen/Das begyndt es allweg zu wetzen wo es bey staynen ist.Das dosig Thier ist des Helf fanttz todt feyndt.Der Helffandt furcht es fast vbel/dann wo es Jn ankumbt/so laufft Jm das Thier mit dem kopff zwischen dye fordern payn/vnd reyst den Helffandt vnden am pauch auff vñ erwürgt Jn/des mag er sich nit erwern.Dann das Thier ist also gewapent/das Jm der Helffandt nichts kan thün.Sie sagen auch das der Rhynocerus Schnell/Fraydig vnd Listig sey.

1515

RHINOCERVS

The Rhinoceros by Albrecht Dürer, 1515, woodcut. The artist had never seen a rhinoceros, but based his animal on verbal descriptions of a gift sent to the King of Portugal which was exhibited in Lisbon. For many years after, other depictions of the rhinoceros copied Dürer's fanciful scales and patterned plates – such was the power of a single print. © The British Museum/ Heriage-Images.

was still searching for a technique that would permit finer detail than was available using wood. He had started copper engraving in 1497 and by 1514 was producing masterpieces like *Melencolia I* and *St Jerome in His Study*. No longer merely illustrations to accompany a text, but intended to be seen as individual pictures, these engravings were acknowledged as outstanding works of art in their own right. Dürer was a pioneer, but he was by no means alone: there were famous schools of etching, engraving and woodcut in Germany, the Low Countries, France and Italy.

However, the majority of printed images, up to the invention of photography, served primarily to educate or amuse, and at the time were not treated as works of art; many have since come to be regarded as such. For example, old maps are now treasured more for their pictorial qualities and technique than for their accuracy of information. The Renaissance created an enormous demand for knowledge in Europe, and woodcuts, etchings and engravings abound on every subject: anatomy, botany, architecture, navigation and medicine. These sciences were all advanced by the exchange of ideas in illustrated form. Illustrated song sheets, stories and calligraphic copying books were all widely popular. Designs for furniture and fashionable clothes promoted a Europe-wide culture, and everywhere the doctrine of Christianity was spread or reinforced by the images of saints and miracles. The value of printed pictures in communicating ideas to a wide but still largely illiterate audience was soon recognised by rulers and politicians, and measures were taken to control sedition by requiring both printer and artist to have their names engraved beneath the image.

The dissemination of artistic ideas

From the early 16th century, paintings and sometimes sculptures were copied in the form of easily portable prints, so that the work of famous Renaissance artists became known throughout Europe. These prints were often anonymous and frequently inaccurate; however, some of the engravers were skilful, and their interpretations of other artists' work have always been highly regarded. Marcantonio Raimondi (1480–1534) born near Bologna, was one such engraver. He became very successful through his engravings after works by Raphael, Michelangelo, Dürer and Titian. Raphael (1483–1520) also employed his own engraver, as did Peter Paul Rubens (1577–1640) a little later, to ensure that the engravings were accurate and did justice to the original work. This was a wise move: at one point Dürer accused Raimondi of copying his works too closely and passing them off as his own.

The search for tonal expression

A further development of etching and engraving was required by both the copyist and the creative printmaker in order to express the widest range of tones from black to white through all the greys. The copyist or reproductive printmaker had the greatest difficulty in interpreting a dramatic painting in full colour in only black and white. To create tone, or degrees of light and shade, printmakers had to make use of an optical illusion: black dots, hatching or similar marks close together create an impression of grey; depending on the size of the marks and their density within an area, the impression would be of a lighter or darker tone. In etching and engraving this could be done by cross-hatching of lines, dots or the thickening of a line, but also by varying the depth of each mark to hold more or less ink.

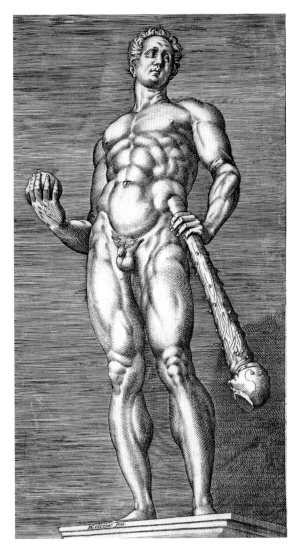

Statue of Hercules by Hendrick Goltzius, c.1592, engraving. This huge statue was unearthed about 1550 in Rome and is probably a Roman copy of a Greek work; Goltzius saw it in 1591. The engraved lines are perfect for expressing the dramatic physique of the statue. © The British Museum/Heritage-Images.

The South Sea Bubble by William Hogarth, 1721, etching and engraving. A satire on the speculators who were caught up in this famous scandal and are shown here on the merry go round. Honour and Honesty are being flogged in the foreground by Self Interest and Villainy.
© Corporation of London/Heritage-Images.

The basic aim in printing is to devise a means of holding the right amount of ink in the right place and transferring it to paper, over and over again. Until colour printing became common, methods of depicting tone exercised the mind of every inventive printmaker and technician. If you take a magnifying glass and look at some old etchings and engravings, you will see how the artist has used these skills to create an illusion.

Rembrandt (1606–69) reached unsurpassed heights of expression and tonal contrast in his black and white etchings; in lesser hands, however, the rendering of tone by means of lines and dots was frequently formalised and pedestrian.

Some artists experimented with chiaroscuro woodcuts to try to extend their tonal range. Lucas Cranach the Elder (1472–1553) in Saxony cut extra woodblocks which he printed in lighter tints over the main design to supplement the range of tones. There was also a demand for ways of imitating the greater freedom of crayon or pencil drawings: thus the 'crayon manner', as it was known, was made up of tiny dots in imitation of the flecks of crayon or graphite pencil on rough paper. However, of much greater importance in the search for increased tonality was the development of first mezzotint and then aquatint.

Mezzotint was invented in Holland around 1640 by Ludwig von Siegen (c. 1609–80) and later developed by Prince Rupert of the Rhine (1619–82). The new technique was brought to England, where it became so popular

that it became known as the 'English manner'. Mezzotint is a method of engraving in which a tool cuts a mark on the plate to hold ink. The technique permits an infinite range of tones from very deep, velvety blacks to pure white. It was widely used for portraits and reproductions, but attracted few creative artists until it was revived in the mid-20th century.

The origins of aquatint are uncertain, but an efficient method was developed in the 1760s, principally by Jean-Baptiste Le Prince (1733–81). Aquatint is a variety of etching which at that time was restricted to the use of lines drawn through a wax coating on the metal plate; when it was put in an acid bath the metal exposed by the drawn lines was etched to a depth which could hold ink. The breakthrough with aquatint was to cover the plate with a dusting of resin that was impervious to the acid; those areas not to be etched were stopped out with varnish brushed on to those parts of the plate. The acid then etched the still-exposed metal around each grain of resin: if etched for a short time, the design would hold little ink and result in a grey tone; if etched for longer and deeper, it made a darker tone. Aquatint was often used in conjunction with line etching, the former for the tone and the latter for the structure of the design. Aquatint was also a quicker method of printmaking than mezzotint, and, though it could not rival the latter's depth of tone, it proved so flexible a medium that it became, and indeed remains, the most popular method of printmaking.

View of Hampstead Heath, Hampstead, London by David Lucas after John Constable, 1832, mezzotint. David Lucas was skilled at interpreting Constable's paintings in the medium of mezzotint. He worked very closely with the artist; these are collaborative prints of the highest quality. The very wide tonal range of mezzotint is demonstrated by this print.
© Corporation of London Libraries and Guildhall Art Gallery.

Print booms

Prints became enormously popular during the 17th and 18th centuries, and as communications improved print publishers became successful businessmen all over Europe. It was common for a publisher to buy a completed plate from an artist and then print from it to satisfy demand. Editions and signatures were unknown: popular plates were printed until they wore down and then frequently re-engraved to strengthen the lines again. The prices of old prints thus can vary a lot according to the condition of the original plate when the print was made.

The Old Masters

Rembrandt, among all the masters of etching, is of special interest to the collector of modern prints. He was in the habit of working on some plates for a long time before they reached a state he considered finished. Each time he made a modification on the copperplate, by adding more lines or burnishing some away, he took a proof; each slightly different proof is known as a state. By looking at a series of states it is possible to see how the artist's idea has developed. Rembrandt's love of experimentation, the way he used all the possibilities the medium offered, is very close to the way artists look at printmaking today. The collecting of state proofs is a special field that appeals to some connoisseurs.

In France, Louis XIV and his courtiers were great patrons of the arts. By around 1660, Cardinal Mazarin is reputed to have had a collection of 120,000 prints, which later became the nucleus of the largest print collection in the world, now housed in the Bibliothéque Nationale in Paris.

Lithography

The invention by Aloys Senefelder (1771–1834), in Munich in 1796, of an entirely new way of printing was to provide artists with a marvellously rich and varied medium, though it took another century to fully develop. Senefelder had spent many years trying to find a cheap method that he could use to print the text of his own plays. He tried variations on etching using slabs of stone instead of expensive copper. By chance, he discovered the principle of lithography, and his experience in other forms of printing enabled him to develop a sound working method as well as a special printing press for the new technique.

Senefelder, who had a ready supply of fine-quality Bavarian limestone, called the new method 'chemical printing', since it is based on the antipathy of grease to water and does not involve engraving the image. His invention was taken to London and then Bath, where the first artists' lithographs were published in 1803. The first lithographic press was set up in America in 1818, where its use was soon widespread. In an equally short period of time, it was used throughout Europe and had been taken by missionaries to India and beyond. Artists still use stone today, though commercial lithography is now done entirely from various metal plates.

The colour explosion

The demand for colour prints was difficult to satisfy until colour lithography became widespread. Multi-block colour woodcuts were tedious to cut, and multi-plate etchings and engravings equally time-consuming and expensive to make. Many colour aquatints were printed from two plates and had patches of colour applied to the plate by hand before printing (a method called *a la poupée*), but this was a slow and skilful process. Most prints were monochrome and were later hand-coloured with watercolour; this was often done by poorly paid gentlewomen whose only alternative employment would be working as governesses.

Lithography could now be used to make larger prints than those available by any other method; though one stone was required for each colour, the stones could be four feet or more in length and the raw material was cheap. Early lithographs imitated drawings, and it was some time before the full range of the medium was understood by artists.

The Three Crosses by Rembrandt van Rijn, 1653, etching. This proof is state IV. The plate has been greatly re-worked with the exception of the figures on the crosses. The other figures have been scraped or burnished and new vertical lines are scored through the sky. Light is dramatically centred on the figure of Christ while darkness envelopes the crowd of centurions and onlookers. © The British Museum/ Heritage-Images.

The Port of Aegina by Paul Sandby, 1777, aquatint. This print shows the painterly textures in imitation of washes which are typical of aquatint. Sandby was well known for his watercolours and he found that aquatint was very sympathetic for his work.
© The British Museum/Heritage-Images.

Illustration

In France lithography was widely used for illustrations. Honoré Daumier (1810–79) produced 4,000 lithographic illustrations for *Le Charivari* and *La Caricature*, for which he is justly famous. British illustrators tended to prefer wood engravings. Engraving on the end grain of boxwood had been widely used for fabric-printing blocks; but it was not taken up by illustrators until Thomas Bewick (1755–1828) realised the potential of the very fine end grain of the wood, on which greater detail could be cut than was possible using the long, plank grain of the traditional woodcut. In addition, wood engravings could be printed together with metal type, which made the printing of illustrated journals, catalogues, books and advertisements very economical. Where speed was important – for example, for reportage from a battle scene or accident – blocks were engraved in sections by several artisans and joined together for printing. By the mid-19th century wood engraving had deteriorated into a purely reproductive technique: though prints from this period often still displayed technical virtuosity, it was not considered a medium for fine art.

The revival of the woodcut

While he was living on Tahiti in the 1890s, the French artist Paul Gauguin (1848–1903) began cutting into whatever wood he could find, usually rough planks. These works were far from the neat, genteel woodcuts of the time; they were bold depictions of Tahitian flora, figures and symbols, and as such they influenced a number of other artists to reconsider the

medium. One of these was Edvard Munch (1863–1944), who believed it was essential to control the making of the print throughout the process and certainly to avoid asking a print technician to do any of the work. He experimented with colour, sometimes cutting up a block like a jigsaw puzzle and colouring each part differently, then putting the bits together for printing. Sometimes he outlined the subject matter with a cut line that would remain white, and then brushed colour onto the different parts, keeping the block whole. Both methods produced multicoloured prints from one block. Also, it was easy to put different colours in different places so that each print represented a new variation.

At around the same time in Germany, the woodcut was the favoured method for graphic work among a group of artists calling themselves *Die Brücke* (The Bridge), founded in 1905 as a protest against dry academicism. Out of *Die Brücke* grew Expressionism; artists saw that the vigour and immediacy of the woodcut was ideal for expressing strong social comment on the state of Europe in the first half of the 20th century.

Abstraction and Cubism

The beginning of the 20th century saw improved communications that enabled artists to travel easily throughout Europe. The traditional training of artists in academies in the painstaking learning of techniques seemed too slow for the pace of the new concepts of the modern movement. Instead, artists turned their hands to whatever medium was available.

Rue Transnonain, le 15 Avril, 1834 by Honoré Daumier, 1834, lithograph, published in 'La Caricature' journal. This very realistic reportage drawing is based on an incident in Paris when government troops shot a family after a riot which had happened ten days earlier. Daumier was a leader against the suppression of political satire.
© The British Museum/ Heritage-Images.

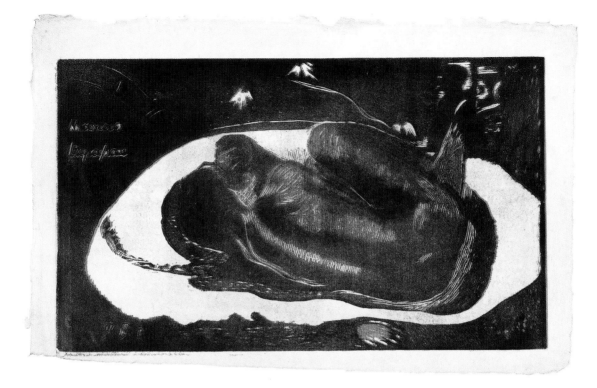

Manao Tupapau (Watched by the Spirits of the Dead) by **Paul Gauguin**, c.1893, woodcut, one of a group of ten known as *Noa Noa (Fragrant Scent)* series. Gauguin was fascinated by the fear of the spirits of the dead which played a large part in the life of the people of Tahiti where he was living. He wrote in a letter to his wife 'I must explain this fear with as few of the time-honoured literary devices as possible'.
© The British Museum/ Heritage-Images.

Where that medium was printmaking, they bypassed the professional engraver and lithographer in their determination to reach a wider public with the new ideas.

In all forms of printmaking, the artist has to take positive decisions. It is never as easy to make alterations to a printing matrix as it is to, say, a painting or drawing. When this decisiveness is practised by artists such as the Cubists, who had an exciting new theory to propound, powerful prints can result. Some of the best early Cubist works by Georges Braque (1882-1963) and Picasso (1881-1973), made around 1911, were line etchings. Equally, in Russia just after the Revolution of 1917, Abstract artists adopted the woodcut and lithograph as a means of disseminating their ideas within Russia and beyond.

École de Paris

Paris, between the two World Wars was the international centre of the art world, and printmaking flourished on an unprecedented scale. Picasso was mostly making etchings at that time, while Henri Matisse (1869–1954), Braque, Joan Miró (1893–1983) and Marc Chagall (1887–1985) preferred lithography. Much of this activity was fostered by publishers and the studios that printed for them. Print workshops such as Mourlot's for lithography and Lacourière's for intaglio were very influential in promoting a high standard of technical excellence, and established a sound pattern for print studios later established all over the world.

Britain and America

British and American artists frequently visited Paris, and adopted Impressionism, Expressionism, Abstraction, Cubism and other 'isms' in their painting and sculpture. Their printmaking, however, remained largely traditional. Monochrome etchings and wood engravings of landscape, architecture and domestic scenes were very popular on both sides of the Atlantic, but curiously, in spite of the fact that colour lithography was first developed in London in the 1830s, it was not used by artists following the example of the French. The market for black and white prints seemed insatiable in the late 1920s, but it completely collapsed after the stock-market crash of 1929.

The isolation of America during the Depression and the desire to avoid involvement with Europe promoted a range of disparate if distinctly American styles. The Federal Arts Project, set up in America during the 1930s, sponsored printmaking as a way of employing artists to make affordable art and thereby fostered the beginning of screenprinting, another new print method.

Postwar renaissance of printmaking

The printmaking workshops of Paris revived quickly after 1945, resuming almost where they had left off with a stream of lithographs, etchings, woodcuts and linocuts. Prints which had been completed just before the occupation but had not been published were luckily rediscovered: the *Vollard Suite* of etchings by Picasso suffered this fate and was finally published in 1950.

This flood of images was marketed internationally, but at the same time several doubtful practices crept in: plates were made by skilful copyists, but the prints were signed by the artist; several editions of the same image were printed; once a famous artist signed a pile of blank paper before the edition had even been printed!

The print galleries which opened in Britain and America at this time started by showing these French prints but soon encouraged indigenous artists to make prints too. Rather than go to the Parisian ateliers, a number of workshops modelling themselves on the French prototype were opened for these new printmakers. The early work produced in these workshops looked to Paris for inspiration, but younger artists were becoming resentful of Paris's domination of the art world and soon moved in different directions; new movements and, naturally, new forms of printmaking were developing.

Screenprinting: Pop and Op Art

The tremendous growth of printmaking in the 1960s has been called a print boom. This seems to imply a short-lived extravaganza and a possible end to the wave of enthusiasm. There have been many temporary fluctuations in the demand for artists' prints that have closely followed the economy: inflation and depression have their effect; the quality of the work has nothing to do with it. In spite of these variations, which of course make life very difficult for artists, there is still widespread and genuine interest in artists' prints for their aesthetic values, not just their investment worth.

This print boom was fostered by the development of the new printing method of screenprinting. Fundamentally, this is a sophisticated form of stencilling that had been revolutionised by technological advances in synthetic materials, developments that had occurred largely during the Second World War. Screenprinting had been used between the wars for poster printing, but now photographic images could be incorporated and the inks had a greater brilliance and opacity. This was ideal for the intense and solid colours required by practitioners of Op (optical) Art and other hard-edge artists. Pop artists, who wanted to collage together fragments of packaging, magazines, illustrations and other elements of everyday life, could at last incorporate photographs.

As a new technique unencumbered by historical precedent, screen-printing was psychologically attractive to artists breaking away from the influence of Paris. The traditional printing methods were still used by many artists, but for a time screenprinting seized the foreground.

New materials, new methods

The lure of experimenting with newly developed materials and techniques has threatened to engulf many printmakers, with the computer being the most alluring of all. It could do things that were previously impossible. An image can be manipulated in size, colour, tiling, layering; it can be made to imitate brushstrokes, pencil, chalk or pen; it can be rendered hard-edged or feathered; it can be merged with another image; it can be solid or screened. The artist can try out a composition in hundreds of variations. In the early days the result of all this experimentation could only be printed through crude digital printers onto office-type paper. These prints were glossy, coarse and very unattractive; they also had a very short life before the colours faded and the paper discoloured. The computer systems used were initially designed for industry, but it was not long before artists found several ways of integrating digital systems with the traditional printing methods of relief, intaglio, lithography and screenprint to produce hybrid prints on the best-quality archival paper and, increasingly, using lightfast inks. The quality of pure digital prints could now also be of the same high standard required by artists' prints.

Printmaking now

Experimentation for its own sake is arid; old or new methods and materials are only justified if their use enhances the idea or image being conveyed. If printing on a transparent surface such as acrylic sheet conveys a certain feeling of space, then choosing that material before paper would seem justified. A sequential movement of line, which has to obey complex rules,

will be more convincing if plotted with the aid of a computer than if it were drawn by hand.

If, however, the choice of method and material seems merely to follow the latest fashion or sensation it will seem superficial in intent. Images have been printed on every possible surface: plastic, metal, ceramic, textiles, three-dimensional moulded forms, book forms and hangings. They have incorporated embossing, collage, flocking, metallic film and cast paper, and been of every shape: circular, square, irregular, extremely small and or simply vast. Many must be treated as ephemeral objects that will not survive because the materials used are not designed to last. They are a nightmare for museum conservationists.

We are now going through a period of consolidation of the experience gained of new materials and methods, and a reappraisal of traditional ways. Computers are no longer an exciting new plaything, but have now become ubiquitous. Most artists have got over their initial excitement and now see them as just another tool in an artist's potential repertoire.

As to the future, commercial printing techniques will inevitably continue changing, and artists will doubtless go on adopting some of them in seeking to advance their art. Printmaking will also invariably continue to exist in many forms, from traditional works on paper to be framed and

Alice (Golden Girl) (part 1 of a triptych) by Mick Kelly, 1999. Overlaid Lazertran waterslide transfer print, 300 x 400 mm (11¾ x 15¾ in). Printed and published by the artist. The artist describes the technique as follows: '*Photocopy the image onto Lazertran waterslide decal and immerse it in water until the decal releases. Paint the paper (the substrate to carry the image) with real turpentine. Apply the decal and overnight the image and the decal migrate into the paper. When dry, a second decal can be applied in the same way as the first.*'

Residue I by Ione Parkin, 2002. Solar etching (photopolymer intaglio) and monotype, 228 x 178 mm (9 x 7 in). Printed and published by the artist. Unique print.

The artist says, *'My work is in a sense a homage to the force of nature ... a finely balanced and sustainable system where each of the complex variety of marks makes a vital and unique contribution to the success of the whole ... Monotype appeals to me as a painter for its immediacy and fluidity. The solar-etching process is appealing on one level for its technical simplicity ... I work on a series of experimental drawings ... there is then the element of surprise in translating from one medium to another [drawing to print].'*

hung on a wall to architectural-scale works for public spaces. It will surely also continue to be combined with other forms, such as installations, videos and book works. Printmaking is always reinventing itself.

Why Do Artists Make Prints?

Artists fall into two camps: some make prints simply to replicate an image as a means of increasing their income and getting their name to a wider public – they are often not much concerned how it is done. The second group gets a great deal of satisfaction from handling the materials used, pushing techniques to their limits, using experimental printmaking as a means of exploring ideas and experiencing what many describe as a magical moment when the print is lifted off the press.

The democratic art

In recent years, artists have looked for new ways to relate to people who care about art but are not collectors in the traditional sense. Painting and sculpture are all too often associated with museums, cathedrals and palaces. So some artists have made video and film their primary medium; others have used everyday materials to create installations and site-specific public sculptures, such as Antony Gormley (b. 1950) with his *Angel of the North* in northern England; others make ephemeral art from leaves, stones and the elements in the landscape; but many have turned to print, which we see everywhere, as surely the medium of modern mass communication – the democratic art.

During the First and Second World Wars the British Ministry of Information commissioned many artists to make lithographic poster prints, and from the 1920s London Underground and Shell-Mex & BP Ltd asked all the leading artists to work in this format. In 1937 and 1938, two series of Contemporary Lithographs were published in editions of 400 by Robert Wellington of the Zwemmer Gallery with technical advice from John Piper (1903–93). Sadly, most copies were lost in the London Blitz. The short-lived venture School Prints Ltd, set up in 1946, commissioned leading British artists such as John Nash (1893–1977) and Henry Moore to produce lithographs that were then editioned in large numbers so that they could be sold cheaply to schools. In 1949, there was even a European series featuring the likes of Picasso, Braque and Matisse. All these poster prints are now collector's items.

So there have been many attempts to democratise art through the use of print. And the production of large quantities of a particular print, thus enabling a cheaper retail price, dispels the whiff of elitism that surrounds the limited edition. Inevitably, if a large number of prints is planned, the use of hand-printing techniques such as intaglio, woodcut and other relief prints, as well as direct lithography, has to be eliminated; these techniques take too long to print, and in any case the surface will often break down after a hundred or so prints. This leaves the long-run methods of offset lithography, screenprinting and more recently digital printing, all of which, sadly, lose the individual touch of hand-printing and are printed on cheaper and rather uninteresting paper. Many attempts have been made, with the best of intentions, to market unlimited editions but, with the exception of selling extremely cheaply in bulk to hotel furnishers, all such

Newhaven Harbour by Eric
Ravilious, 1937. Lithograph, 540
x 770 mm (21¼ x 31¼ in).
Published by Contemporary
Lithographs in an edition of
400, signed on the plate, not
numbered.

schemes have failed. Lyons tea shops commissioned prints for their cafes
in the 1950s, as did the brewers Guinness for their pubs; and the print
publishers Curwen and Editions Alecto both unsuccessfully issued
unlimited editions during the 1960s.

Artists' posters (for their own exhibitions) and poster poems
(collaborations between a poet and an artist) have often been printed in
quite large numbers using commercial printing techniques, and they
seemed to have fared somewhat better: calling something a poster puts it
in a recognised category, whereas unlimited editions are suspect. It seems
the value of art is inextricably linked to its rarity, and so artists working in
print continue to make limited editions smaller or larger depending on the
demand for their work and their own philosophy.

Motivation: artists who make prints

Artists who want to replicate their ideas using print primarily as a means of
earning a living are frequently encouraged to do so by a gallery or dealer,
and as such they usually do not call themselves printmakers. If they have
built an international reputation as a painter, sculptor, installation artist or
site-specific artist, they may not produce enough work to satisfy demand
or the work may relate to a particular place. Both the artist and the gallery
or dealer need an income source to support the main work – hence they

Frank Stella preparing an assembled plate for the *Swan Engraving* series, assisted by Kenneth Tyler at the Tyler Graphics Ltd workshop, November 1981. Photograph by Lindsay Green.

turn to prints. Prints can be produced in quantity for the less wealthy admirer and are a means of widening the audience for an artist's ideas. In contemporary art the ideas and philosophy of the artist matter more than the medium in which they are presented. As a result, the last 40 years have seen some of the most elaborate prints ever produced. Not only has the number of colours printed risen since the mid-1960s, but the size of prints has increased. Other materials have been incorporated, such as metallic foils, flocking and other papers, and different media have been combined in what are usually described as mixed-media prints. These prints have been produced in professional editioning studios, where a master printer guides the artist at every step and sometimes collaborates with them to make the printing matrices. The master printer does all the printing and extra finishing required, such as collage, folding or the addition of handwork. These prints are the product of collaboration and are usually quite expensive.

Galleries with costly premises to maintain find prints as part of their marketing strategy are a useful adjunct to the artist's main work; but, as they are relatively inexpensive, print sales do not contribute hugely to the budget. In recent years many galleries have encouraged artists as a compromise to make monotypes or monoprints. These prints use some of the same techniques as other forms of printmaking and are quite quick to make. Above all from the buyer's point of view a monoprint is a unique image, and thus a gallery can command a higher price for one of these than for a print taken from an edition.

Motivation: printmakers who make art

'Printmakers' are happy to be given this generic title, even though it is still used pejoratively wherever old ideas of 'prints as reproductions and not

Sonnets 55–57 by Simon Brett RE, 1989. Wood engraving 92 x 75mm (3¾ x 3 in). Printed and published by the artist in an edition of 60.

This is a classic wood-engraved illustration with fine detail and a strong literary connection. As a mysterious poetic image it also works as an image for the wall. It alludes to time motifs, the imagery of winter and ocean, and the gilded monuments in three of Shakespeare's sonnets as well as to the fourteen lines of the sonnet itself – the 'eternal lines', as another poem puts it, in which here 'shall you pace forth' in that stride. The artist has made play with the white of the page, which enters through the broken vignetted edge. The image engages with the space around it; the page is more than just its support.

fine art' cling on in the art world and elsewhere. True printmakers take delight in the materials they use; in the best practitioners there is also a close integrity between the idea and the production method of a particular work. There have been many artists who started making prints when urged to do so by their gallery and, even when they had no previous experience of the methods used, came to appreciate the skills of the master printers in professional editioning studios, and found themselves completely entranced by printmaking. For example, Joan Miró said, 'For me engraving is a major means of expression. It has been a means of liberation, expansion and discovery'; and Marc Chagall said, 'It seems to me that something would have been lacking for me if, in addition to colour, I had not at one time in my life, worked at engraving and lithography', and 'whenever I bent over the lithography stone … it was as though I was touching a talisman. It seemed as though I could pour all my sadness and joy into it'.

The end product, the print, embodies a respect for the nature of the copper, wood or other material being used, as well as for the struggle to get the inanimate substance to produce what the artist holds in their mind's eye. Henri Matisse said of his linocuts, 'I have often thought that this simple medium is comparable to the violin with its bow … The gouge, like the violin bow, is in direct rapport with the feelings of the engraver' – and, what's more, he was a fine violin player. Printmakers have a real love for their materials: they will drool over a specimen book of fine papers; or, having selected a piece of wood, they will use its grain and figuration in their image; or they will spend hours grinding down a piece of lithographic stone until they feel they know its structure intimately.

They also have a reverence for their equipment: a good press is handed down through the generations, and the previous artists who used it are remembered. Traditional Japanese woodcut artists used to spend a couple of years of their apprenticeship learning how to sharpen their knives and gouges alone. These craft skills are not properly taught today: colleges rely on sending tools away to be sharpened and they have to employ technicians to maintain the presses.

For some printmakers, the intellectual challenge is what excites them: working out a plan for the different stages of making a print; envisioning that a black mark will become white and that the left hand of a plate prints the right hand on paper; learning how to use the minimum number of printed colours, which by overprinting will create the full colour range required. Other printmakers are excited by the actual marks, unique to

printmaking, that can be made: an etched line can be finer than any drawn by pen or brush; mezzotint and aquatint give such a velvety texture, you can almost stroke it; a soft ground line is slightly squidgy; a knife-cut line is sharp and precise but still different when cut into a hard wood or soft rubber. Lithography has some of its own special textures, such as the descriptive name given to a particular type of wash: *peau de crapaud* (skin of a toad). Then there is the 3-D effect of deep embossing, the texture of printing from cork, the imprint of a leaf in soft ground or transferred to a litho plate, and above all the huge variety of papers which can be used, from smoothly coated card to the roughest of village papers made by hand in the Himalayas.

Printmakers usually work on their own, but many as members of print collectives share equipment such as presses, acid baths, computers and so on. Such groups also arrange exhibitions of their members' work, either in independent galleries or on their own premises. They exchange exhibitions with other groups at home and abroad. They often have websites, publish catalogues, give classes in printmaking techniques and hold open days. The more sophisticated among these groups also publish their members' work and act as agents; all of them are devoted to encouraging an understanding of printmaking.

Two Miners by Josef Herman, 1962. Lithograph, 580 x 810 mm (23 x 32 in). Printed and published by Curwen Prints Ltd in an edition of 50.
The black is drawn on stone and the brown and yellow on zinc plates.

from the
walk through the
through the field
is soft as the breast
the touch

SECTION TWO

Anger by Wendy Batt, 2002. Relief print, 430 x 300mm (16⅞ x 11¾ in). Printed and published by the artist as part of the Bath Artist Printmakers group millennium project based on the story of Saul and David.
The artist has taken the text *'And Saul cast a javelin at him to smite him; so Jonathan arose from the table in fierce anger'* as the theme. The image is printed from card, lino, rubber stamps and wooden type seen on the left of the finished print.

How Prints Are Made

Printing methods can be divided into five basic categories in order of historical development: relief, intaglio, lithographic, screen and digital. All were initially invented to produce commercially printed books, newspapers, catalogues, posters and cards for the general market, but artists saw that they had qualities which could also be harnessed to make fine art. Today, there is no commercial relief or intaglio printing any more; these methods now belong only to artists and private presses. The majority of commercial printing today is lithographic, whereas screenprinting activity has significantly diminished; in the near future many varieties of digital printing will probably predominate. Then perhaps some new method will be invented – methods will always change.

The specialised terms used here are all explained in more detail in the glossary. Those readers who are really intrigued by the printmaking processes should look at the series of manuals (Printmaking Handbooks) for practising printmakers published by A&C Black.

Opposite:
Orange Study by Olive Webb, 2002. Mixed-media print, 510 x 360 mm (20 x 14⅛ in). Printed and published by the artist. Unique image.
The artist uses print with drawing and collaged papers, some of which are printed from an intaglio acrylic plate and photocopied text.

Relief printing

The printing block or matrix has all the printing areas in relief. All the non-printing parts are cut away or at least should be much lower so that they do not pick up ink from a roller or inking pad. Paper is then laid on the inked block and pressure applied by means of a press or by hand-burnishing. When the paper is lifted off, the ink has been transferred to the paper. This process is repeated for each impression.

Relief-printing blocks can be made from any flat material such as wood, lino, vinyl sheet, card, board, metal sheet, acrylic, photopolymeric plastics and rubber (these last two in a method known as flexography). Blocks can also be made by gluing flat materials such as lace, string, pressed-out metal parts such as washers and other flat found objects onto a stout backing sheet.

Many common tools such as knives and chisels are used to cut away non-printing areas. Specially-made tools are required for wood engraving and similar techniques, but less fine ones are used for woodcutting and linocutting. Some materials can be cut in broad shapes by scissors. Metal plates for relief printing can be hand-cut, but are usually etched in acid or, more likely these days, by digital routing or engraving machines. Photographic elements can be incorporated by exposing a negative, with a dot screen on the tonal areas, to the light-sensitive surface of metal or photopolymer plates.

Alterations to blocks are usually difficult to effect, so the design has to be carefully planned; it has also to be cut in reverse so that when it is printed it reads the right way. Normally, one block is printed for each colour, but if the colours are sufficiently separated, several can be put on one block and each coloured ink applied by small rollers or dabbers. Blocks can also be cut up like a jigsaw puzzle, each bit inked separately and then all the pieces brought together to be printed once. There is another method using only one block called either

Cutting lino – the hands of Katie Clemson RE. She has roughly drawn guidelines on the lino and is then freely cutting using a V-gouge.

Left:
Untitled by Leanne Callender, 2004. Chine-collé linocut. The light-blue areas are torn strips of blue paper overprinted in a darker blue. The artist was a student at Barking College, London.

Below:
Weir on the River Dove at Wolfscotdale by Rosemary Simmons HonRE, 1975. Relief print from plywood, etched and cut lino and found scrap wood, 407 x 580 mm (16 x 22¾ in). Printed in five colours on an 1868 Albion press and published by the artist in an edition of 25.

reduction, or elimination, or 'suicide print'. All white areas are removed and the first colour is printed. The block is then cleaned, more material is cut away and another print is taken. This process is repeated until the final image is complete.

Asian relief prints have traditionally been printed with water-based colours from wood, whereas the Western tradition is to use oil-based inks with all block materials. Water-soluble inks have recently been developed for Western relief printing. Relief blocks print better on soft paper (paper not treated with size or glue, or else with very little) and can also be printed on dampened or dry paper. Asian prints are traditionally printed using a pressure pad held in the hand, whereas Western prints make use of a press when available, though some Western artists use hand-burnishing by means of the back of a wooden spoon or similar object. Presses vary from old 19th-century models to newly-made presses, and can be either large, floor-standing machines or smaller tabletop designs.

Characteristics of relief prints

In general, relief prints are bold and sharp. Lines resemble a pen-and-ink drawing more than those of a pencil drawing; there are no halftones unless these are created on a photoplate. Printed areas are usually solid, though there are also tricks for

Marcus Aurelius VII by Simon Brett RE, 2002. Wood engraving, 151 x 90 mm (6 x 3 ½ in). Printed and published by the artist in an edition of 60. The artist says, 'This is one of a series of 13 illustrations for the Folio Society edition of The Meditations of Marcus Aurelius (2002). The images, which are based on photographs of sculptural likenesses of the Emperor, are arranged to circle around the head and are conceived as a meditation upon his ageing, that of the stone or bronze of which they are made, and upon the sculptural style, from Hellenistic towards Romanesque. They are translated into the marks and shapes and tones of wood engraving in various ways.'

blotting off some of the colour from the block or for varying areas of pressure when printing by hand; lino can also be etched to lend the print a grainy texture. Asian printers also sometimes use the grain of the wood or paper to diffuse water-based inks by capillary action.

The material of the printing block influences the marks made on the paper. Coarse-grained wood, i.e. cut along the length of the tree, used in woodcuts shows up as slightly ragged edges to the cut marks, or else the grain itself shows up when printed; these qualities are exploited by artists to create drama and texture. Wood can also be textured by wire-brushing and by weathering. Wood engraving is a much finer art and uses the cross grain of woods such as box and some fruit-tree woods, giving a very fine level of detail in cutting. Asian woodblocks are traditionally made from cherrywood cut along the grain, but the wood is sufficiently fine-grained to give great detail as we know from the evidence of prints by the great masters such as Katsushika Hokusai (1760–1849) and Ando Hiroshige (1797–1858).

Modern materials such as lino, vinyl and rubber cut cleanly, but some people think that the mark looks mechanical in comparison to woodcut; their advantage is that they can be cut in any direction without the influence of a grain, and they can also print large areas of flat colour particularly well. Card and board give their own marks – hard-edged when cut, but soft-edged when indented – or they print their own characteristic textures when inked, such as those you can get from corrugated paper or scrunched-up tissue paper. Photopolymer materials allow blocks to be made using a negative image, drawn or photographic, on film. It is only possible to print the uppermost surface of most natural found objects, such as the raised veins of leaves, unless special printing methods are used.

Terms associated with relief prints

Relief prints are also called surface or block prints. The material of the printing block gives its name to the subdivision in the genre: woodcut, wood engraving; linocut, lino engraving, lino etching; cardboard or Masonite® cut; Perspex,® Plexiglas,® or acrylic cut; card print, rubber, vinyl or Stenocut; relief photopolymer print. Flexography is used for commercial printing from photo-relief blocks made from rubber or photopolymeric materials, but nowadays it is also used by artists printing from similar blocks. Prints from blocks made of collaged materials are usually called mixed-media prints or relief collagraphs.

The term 'white line' describes a design that is predominantly white on a black background, and is mainly associated with wood engraving or very fine-line linocuts. Relief etchings are made from metal plates etched in acid but surface-printed instead of intaglio-printed. Relief etchings that incorporate photographic elements would in the past have been called process engravings; now we would call them photo-relief etchings.

'Letterpress' is a general term for commercial relief printing from metal type and process engraving or photomechanical line blocks. It is now almost defunct, though small specialist private presses still print from type and type-high wood engravings or mounted lino blocks.

Tower of Pisa, perhaps by Anne Desmet RE, 2002. Relief print with collage and pencil, 233 × 111 mm (9¼ x 4⅜ in). The artist says that '*The collage includes Italian banknotes, and marbling, and the print is from wood engraving and linocut. It is assembled on a painted MDF panel and is also unique.*'

Intaglio printing

Still Life in Silence II by
Bartolomeu dos Santos RE,
1992. Etching and aquatint, 593
x 655 mm (23⅝ x 25 in).
Printed and published by the
artist.
This freely rendered version of
a traditional still life and frame
exploits the wide tonal range
and the textures of intaglio. The
lower part is inked in a brown
ink, giving a sense of
foreground; though it is printed
in two colours, it goes through
the press only once.

The printing plate has the image incised on it (intaglio). All the printing parts must be below the surface of the plate. Ink is rubbed into the incised design and then cleaned off the plate surface with a stiff cloth, such as scrim, and finally with the ball of the hand or a piece of tissue. Dampened paper is laid on the inked plate and high pressure applied by means of a press. When the paper is lifted off the ink has been transferred to it from the plate. This process is repeated for each impression.

Intaglio printing plates are usually made from sheet metal; copper, zinc and steel are the commonest. Copper is generally preferred because it is more malleable than the other metals, and therefore easier to rework if corrections have to be made. Acrylic sheet is often used for drypoints, and printing plates also can be made by collaging materials onto a metal or acrylic backing sheet (see *collagraph* and *hybrid systems*). Photographic elements can be incorporated on light-sensitive etching or photopolymer plates by exposing a negative or positive, with a dot screen on the tonal areas.

Two principal methods are used to incise the design into the plate surface: acid is used to etch the design and engraving tools to cut, scratch and indent the plate. There are many formulae for the acid bath, which depend on the metal used and the speed of etching required. Nitric and hydrochloric were once the most commonly used acids, but for safety reasons these have largely been replaced by ferric chloride (technically a salt). Electrolysis is used by some artists. The basic method is to cover any non-printing areas with an acid-resisting coat of wax or varnish, or

Jumbo Jet – Shaking by Anne Breivik, 1976. Engraving on copper, 290 x 210 mm (11⅜ x 8¼ in). Printed and published by the artist.

The artist says, 'The engraving is part of a book, Memories of a Landscape, *from 1976. It's my memory of a journey by jumbo jet from Colorado to Chicago. I remember that the plane, the first jumbo jet ever, was shaking all the way over the flat land. I was afraid that it would fall apart and leave us all scattered over the landscape. There is a text written by Jon Bing following this image. It says, "The atmosphere was built up of thin, thin plates of glass which were splintered by the heavy body of the plane. We are in an alien realm: the transparent landscape of the air."'*

with a photoresist, and then to expose the printing areas to the acid in a tray or bath. The plate can be bitten to varying depths to hold more or less ink: a shallow incision prints lighter than a deeply incised area.

Both plates made by etching or electrolysis and plates made by various engraving methods can be corrected to some extent by burnishing and reworking. The design has to be drawn in reverse so that it reads the right way when printed. There are several ways of making colour prints – for example, either using one plate per colour or inking several colours on one

Squeezing Lemons by Anita Klein PRE, 2003. Drypoint on aluminium, 410 x 305 mm (16 x 12in). Printed and published by the artist in an edition of 25.

plate (see the section on *colour printing*). Printing ink is traditionally oil-based, though water-based inks are now being developed for artists concerned about health and safety. Paper is usually printed damp so that it can be sucked into the incised lines of the plate and pick up the ink; it is sized in order to strengthen it during dampening and printing. Intaglio presses – also called copperplate, roller or etching presses – have to be pretty substantial machines so that they can give the necessary five tons pressure per square inch. Hand-printing is not an option with intaglio.

Characteristics of intaglio prints

In general, intaglio prints rely on fine drawing and texture more than on colour. The most obviously recognisable characteristic is the impressed edge of the metal plate and the slight embossment of all inked lines. Old intaglio prints were sometimes trimmed into the plate area, so the plate-mark is no longer there. Be aware that some reproductions are given false plate-marks by embossing so as to mimic an intaglio print. The depth of intaglio embossing depends on whether the damp printed paper has been dried under weight or stretched by fixing the edges. It also depends on the type of paper used: a heavy paper holds the deformation better.

The quality of the line or texture reveals how the plate was made: the engraved line is crisp and controlled; the etched line, on the other hand, is slightly irregular and freer, as the drawing needle is offered no resistance by the wax resist. Mezzotint shows a slightly criss-cross texture in the midtones, whereas aquatint shows an all-over irregular pattern. Extremely fine lines made by etching or engraving are finer than any pen, pencil or brush mark. Larger areas of ink can only be held on the plate prior to printing by means of a texture made by aquatint, mezzotint, a photo-halftone screen or closely incised lines.

Terms associated with intaglio prints

Intaglio prints are also called 'copperplate prints', and the words 'gravure' and 'engraving' are frequently used indiscriminately for all forms of intaglio prints. The particular way an intaglio print is produced also gives its name to each of the various subdivisions of the genre. Using acid to bite the design into the printing plate gives line or hard-ground etching, soft-ground etching, aquatint, lift-ground aquatint and photo-etching. Photopolymer print refers to the light-sensitive plastic material of the

Once upon a Time the Paradise Was Lost by Carmen Gracia RE, 1977. Etching and welded copper wire, 710 x 560 mm. (28 x 22 in). Printed and published by the artist.
The artist says, 'My method is to cut multiple plates of irregular shapes and amalgamate them, at times by superimposition, thus forming the final image on the bed of the press. I etch the surface, using a traditional ground and needle, then bite it in nitric acid, preferring deeply bitten lines and adding soft-ground textures. Sometimes I ink copper wire to obtain a line or an image.'

plate. The making of a plate without the use of acid is called engraving, drypoint, mezzotint, carborundum, collagraph or digital intaglio. Embossed prints, inked or printed blind (uninked), are usually printed on an intaglio press, though the matrix may be wood, lino, metal or collaged materials and so may fall into the intaglio category. The action of the tools further describes the quality of the line or texture: hence, needling in line etching, burnishing in mezzotint, and aquatint or burin in engraving.

'Photogravure' is a term used for commercial intaglio printing but, as that has now been largely superseded by lithography, the term is used by artists to mean a form of photo-etching where the biting is closely controlled by the artist.

Lithographic printing

In lithography, the printing surface has the image chemically embedded in it. The image is greasy and the non-image areas are water-absorbent. Ink is rolled onto the surface and adheres only to the greasy areas, being repelled by the damp, non-printing parts; the surface is alternately sponged with water and rolled with ink. Paper is laid on the matrix and pressure applied by means of a press. When the paper is lifted the ink has been transferred to the paper. This process is repeated for each impression.

The printing surface is traditionally a slab of limestone of a very fine quality, but alternative, grained metal plates of zinc or aluminium are now common. After printing, the image on stones can be ground down and the stones reused; zinc plates can also be regrained. Each material has its own characteristics: metal plates are lighter in weight, but many artists prefer working on stone.

The printing image is drawn or painted on the stone or plate using a greasy chalk or a greasy ink. The image can also be transferred from another surface such as an inked leaf or piece of fabric; from an impression in greasy ink from metal or wood type, an intaglio or relief plate; or from a drawing on lithographic transfer paper. Photographic elements can be incorporated by exposing a negative or positive image on film, with a dot (or stochastic) screen on the tonal areas, to a light-sensitive coating on a plate. The image is then treated with chemicals to fix it into the stone or plate surface. A recent development in commercial printing is called 'waterless

Torrent by Margaret Sheaff, 2000. Lithograph on zinc plate, 500 x 600mm (19¾ x 23⅝in). Printed and published by the artist in an edition of four.

Phoebus by Rosura Jones (aka Rosemary Simmons HonRE), 1965. Offset lithograph, 460 × 610 mm (18 × 24 in). Printed and published by Curwen Prints Ltd in the Unicorn series of unlimited editions.

lithography'; it entails putting a silicone coating on the non-printing areas to repel ink. Some artists have refined this method for printmakers.

Limited alterations can be made to stone, fewer to zinc and, with difficulty, to aluminium. Generally, one stone or plate is required for each colour. There are two methods of printing: on the traditional direct press the paper is placed directly on the inked matrix and so the image has to be reversed in order that it reads the right way when printed. The second method is called 'offset lithography'. Developed for faster commercial printing, it has the advantage for artists that the ink is transferred onto an offset roller and then onto the paper, so the image on the plate can be seen the right way round from the beginning. The printing ink used is oil- or rubber-based; unsized or lightly-sized papers print best.

Characteristics of lithographic prints

Lithographs usually show brush marks and textures comparable to drawings and paintings; lithography is considered the most painterly of the printmaking techniques. Printing inks are usually transparent, so one colour printed on top of another will give a third where they overlap – for example, red printed on top of blue will give a purple. The whiteness of paper reflects through thin colours giving brilliant hues; a tinted paper will likewise influence the visual result. Furthermore, the inks printed by offset lithography are thinner than those printed on a direct press.

The quality of the line or texture reveals how the plate was made: liquid drawing ink (called 'tusche') used on a brush looks painterly on the paper; used on a pen the result looks like a pen drawing. It can also be spattered, dripped or sponged; if diluted it looks like a watercolour wash,

Space & Space/99D by Susumu Endo, 1999. Lithograph, 440 × 620 mm (17 ¼ × 24 ⅜ in). Printed by the artist in collaboration with a master printer and published by the artist in an edition of 75.
The artist says that he does many sketches in search of composition possibilities and also takes photographs of landscape. Only one single photographic source image is used for each particular lithograph. He then manipulates the image with Adobe Photoshop software in an Apple Mackintosh computer. The image is output on separation films for each colour; usually either five or seven colours are used. He does the printing on a flatbed offset proof press, working manually with the print technician with whom he has collaborated for 20 years.

or mixed with turpentine it looks like marbling. Solid litho chalk or crayon can be anything from 'hard', giving pencil-like lines, to 'very soft', giving a pastel-like mark. It can also be rubbed, shaded and smeared onto the plate. Greasy marks can also be made with ballpoint pens and fingerprints. An even wider range of continuous-tone marks can be made on transparent drawing film, which can then be transferred by exposing the film to a light-sensitive plate. The printing paper is usually smaller than the stone or plate so there is rarely a plate-mark. Printing is done on dry paper, either unsized or only lightly sized.

The King's Tomb by Brian Rice, 1995. Lithograph, 460 × 685 mm (18 × 27 in). Printed and published by the artist in an edition of 65.
By the 1990s the artist had moved away from the hard-edged work of the 60s (see p12) and developed his lifelong interest in archaeology and, in particular, the prehistoric rock carvings and megalithic tombs.

Spiral Shrine by Paul Croft, 1995. Lithograph on aluminium plates, 760 x 560 mm (30 x 22 in), bleed print (printed to the paper edges, no margins). Printed by the artist at the Tamarind Institute, USA and published by Hastings Hotels for the Europa Hotel, Belfast in an edition of 20.
The artist says, *'It was printed from two ball-grained aluminium plates drawn with lithographic crayon and tusche wash (spattered over paper masks). Plate one was printed using a blend of yellow through to pink and plate two was printed in dark-olive ochre.'*

Terms associated with lithographic prints

Lithographs are sometimes referred to as lithos. The materials used give their names to the subdivisions of the genre: stone, plate, direct, offset, transfer, and diazo (another word for continuous tone) lithography. Auto-lithography was once used to describe artist-drawn prints as opposed to those drawn by a copyist (also called a *chromiste* or a chromolithographer). The textural effects are also used to describe prints: drawn, crayon, wash or tusche lithographs. The French word *lavis* is also used to describe wash effects. Photolitho and offset are general terms for commercial printing.

Screenprinting

The printing screen is a finely woven textile stretched on a rectangular frame which supports an impermeable stencil. The open mesh of the textile constitutes the image, and the stencil seals the mesh in non-printing areas. The paper is placed beneath the screen and printing ink is pushed from one end of the screen to the other by a squeegee. Ink comes through the open mesh of the image areas and is deposited on the paper below.

Screen textiles are woven from silk, synthetic fibres or metal, though cheap student experiments can be done with cotton organdie. The frame is made from wood or metal. Stencils are of three basic types: screen fillers, sheet stencils and photographic stencils. Screen fillers are either liquid (varnish, paste, glue) or solid (crayon and wax), each one giving a

Christmas Card by Kip Gresham, 2003. Screenprint, 130 × 175mm. (5 ⅛ × 6 ¾ in). Printed by the artist in five colours, not signed or numbered.

slightly different effect as it fills the spaces within the mesh. Sheet stencils are cut from paper, sheet shellac, plastic sheet or tape, and are stuck on the screen to seal large areas. Photographic stencils are either direct or indirect. The first requires a light-sensitive coating on the screen which is then exposed to a negative or positive photograph and developed. The second uses a photographic negative exposed to a light-sensitive emulsion carried on a plastic sheet, which is developed and transferred onto the screen. A dot (or random) screen must be used in tonal areas. It is easier to make alterations to drawn or cut stencils than to photoscreens. The design is not reversed on the screen.

Printing inks are very versatile and can be oil-, water- or plastic-based, and either opaque or transparent. Almost any type of paper, textile, metal, plastic or wood can be screenprinted. Fine details require a fine mesh and a smooth surface, but there are few other restrictions.

Screenprinting tables can range from the simplest wooden screen hinged along one edge to a flat board, to very large mechanised and digitally-controlled printing machines. The squeegee, which is used to push the printing ink along the screen, is a flexible strip of rubber held in a wooden handle or metal frame, and is just slightly less wide than the inside of the screen frame. Large manual screens will need one person at

Abba Zabba Red by Anthony Frost, 2001. Screenprint with woodblock. Printed and published by Advanced Graphics London in an edition of 75.

A Song for Bill & Kim by Kip Gresham, 2003. Screenprint, 465 x 520 mm (18 ¼ x 20 ½ in). Printed by the artist and published by the Print Studio, Cambridge in an edition of 20.

each end of the squeegee, but most artists' screenprints can be printed by one person. No pressure is required in printing, just an even consistent pull.

Characteristics of screenprints

In general, screenprints are particularly suited to large areas of flat colour, the incorporation of photographic images and, using opaque inks, the complete covering of dark colours by lighter ones. Early screenprint inks were thick, and a three-dimensional deposit of ink could be seen at the printed edges; today, inks can be of almost any consistency. Metallic and fluorescent inks are more successful when screenprinted, having greater density than other methods. Screenprints can be extremely large by comparison with traditional printmaking methods, and they are thus ideal for large modern buildings.

The quality of the printed mark reveals how the screen stencil was made. Direct working on the screen with a brush and liquid screen filler gives a painterly effect; wax crayon gives a coarse drawing texture. The structure of the woven mesh of the screen can be seen as an irregular edge in direct work. Cut stencils give a crisp edge, but detailed work is limited by the flexibility of the knife cut. Photographic stencils give much finer detail to all types of work – drawing, washes and complex textures, as well as actual photographic images.

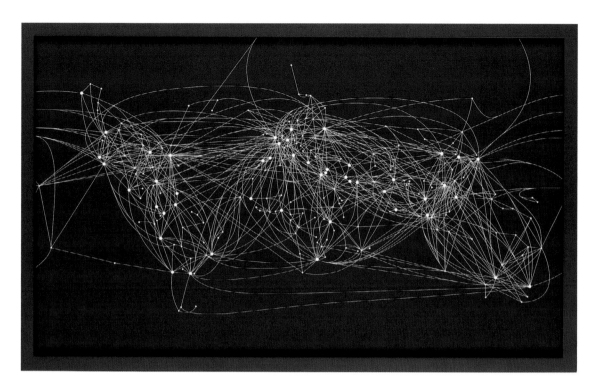

A characteristic of screenprints is the use of many diverse elements which are assembled together: drawings, calligraphy, type, transfers and photographs – almost any visual material can be incorporated both manually and photographically.

Air Routes of the World (Night) by Langlands and Bell, 2001. Screenprint, 840 x 1438 mm (33 x 56 ½ in). Published by the Alan Cristea Gallery in an edition of 45. Reproduced by kind permission of the Alan Cristea Gallery.

Terms associated with screenprints

Screenprints are also called serigraphs, silk-screens, sieve prints and retigraphs. The term 'serigraphy' was used by artists in the early days to differentiate their hand-drawn work on silk textile screens from commercial screenprinting. 'Screenprint' is the universal term used now, though Americans still use 'silk-screen' even though screens are now made of more-reliable synthetic fabrics. Hand-stencilling using stencils cut out of thin metal sheet or card unsupported by a screen belongs to the same genre and is called *pochoir*. In the early 20th century it was a popular method of adding colour to short-run printing of illustrated books and posters; it is occasionally used by artists today. Posterisation is a method by which the colours in a colour photograph or painting can be analysed and interpreted without the use of a halftone screen. The original is photographed or scanned into the four standard process colours of CMYK (cyan, magenta, yellow and black), each in three tones: underexposed, normal and overexposed. The effect of printing in 12 colours (which may be modifications of the process colours) is very rich by comparison with standard colour reproduction.

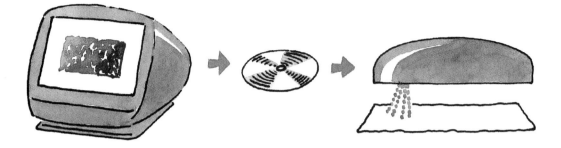

Digital printmaking

Digital printing is a completely new way of originating and then printing an image, and as such requires quite different skills from those used in traditional printmaking. The all-digital image is created and stored by electronic means, which can then give instructions to a digital printer. Thus, in contrast to other forms of printmaking, the artist's physical involvement in making the print is minimal.

Early digital prints were usually printed on small dot-matrix office printers on paper supplied by the manufacturers. The colour was crude, the surface appeal was shiny, the colours were fugitive, and the paper quickly discoloured and crumbled; nothing was up to the standard expected in a work of art. As the technology improved, artists sought ways of using better-quality materials, so that today the main printing system is the ink-jet printer using archival inks on artists' papers.

Constellation (Boat) by Paul Coldwell, 2002. Digital ink-jet print, 540 x 620 mm (21 ¼ x 24 ⅜ in). Printed by Barbara Rauch as part of the Integration of Computers within Fine Art Practice research project at the University of the Arts, London and published by the artist in an edition of seven.

The artist says, '*This is one of a series of eight constellations which explore photographic images in contrast to drawn elements. The objects in the background are sculptures made by the artist. The constellation was made by enlarging some of the dots on the halftone [background] and then joining them up to form, in this case, an image of a boat.*'

The ink-jet printer releases ink in drops onto the paper beneath. Normally, the printers have four standard colours, CMYK (cyan, magenta, yellow and black), which combine optically to produce a wide spectrum of colours; but more sophisticated machines may have six or more colour reservoirs, allowing even greater subtlety.

Another form of digital printmaking requires the image, or perhaps part of the image, to be digitally created. Then, instead of printing it out digitally, the image is printed in black onto film so that it can be used to make printing matrices for photo-relief, photo-etching, photolitho or photoscreen. The digital information can also guide a digital router or engraver, a pen plotter, or a very large-scale ink-jet printer onto textile (theatre backdrops), paper (hoardings) or other materials.

Computers run on programs that allow for a wide variety of marks to be made. These marks can look very like drawings done with pencil, chalk, ink, brush, pen or airbrush, or they can assume draughtsman-like mechanical shapes. Parts of images can be scanned from photographs, paintings, drawings and natural objects, and input into the computer. These elements of the design can then be manipulated in various ways: colours can be changed; edges can be softened or hardened, cut, made irregular; particular elements can be turned in a circle, flipped, copied or tiled. Textures can be superimposed on each other, turning a flat area of colour into one patterned with stars, for example. A feature of modern art is the desire to bring many diverse images together in the manner of a collage; digital imaging does this with the greatest of ease.

"*Princess Dancing.*"   anne Breivik -90

Princess Dancing by Anne Breivik, 1990. Digital print, 160 x 200 mm (6 ¼ x 7 ⅞ in). Printed by the artist.

Characteristics of digital prints

Digital prints are able to mimic most kinds of marks and thus have very few characteristics of their own. However, telling signs are an exceptionally wide spectrum of colours, the manipulation of photographic images, and the multilayering and repetition of parts of the image. Computer prints, done on PCs and standard printers, frequently show slab-shaped pixels without magnification and are likely to have been printed on cheap, non-archival papers. Ink-jet prints show visible signs of pixels or dots of colour under magnification, but other, less common

Untitled CH I by Sue Gollifer, 2002. Iris Print (*giclée*), 482 × 482 mm (19 × 19 in). Image created in Adobe Photoshop and Bryce.

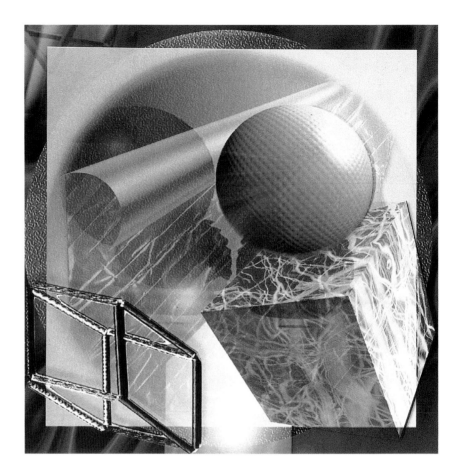

methods of digital printing such as dye sublimation will more closely resemble continuous-tone brilliant photographs. In short, any effect which cannot be achieved by traditional means should suggest digital origination.

Terms associated with digital prints

Ink-jet prints are also called *giclée* prints, from the French verb *gicler* meaning 'to spray'. As the term is used for artist's original ink-jet prints as well as reproductions caution is required before buying any 'print' bearing this description. The term 'computer print' is too vague and suggests a commercial print rather than an artist's print. The name of the printer's manufacturer is also used; hence an 'Iris print' is produced by extremely expensive machines made by an American firm named Iris Graphics, which have been improved to give artist-quality results. Digital etching, digital relief, digital litho and digital screen indicate that, while the printing matrix has been made using some digitally originated material, the final printing method is traditional.

Variations on the Basic Methods

Hybrid, mixed-media and experimental prints

Hybrid prints take the technology from one discipline to use in or adapt to another; examples would be monotypes (not monoprints), collotypes, collagraphs (see Glossary for details on these prints), collaged prints (prints with some material, printed or not, stuck on to the print), partly digital prints, hand-coloured prints and certain transfer prints.

'Mixed media' can be a catch-all definition, and ideally a potential buyer should be able to ask for a more precise account of how a particular print was made. Each method of printing has its own characteristics and sometimes more than one method is needed to realise a particular piece: if

Black Pagoda (for Joan Baez) by Michael Rothenstein RA, 1969. Woodcut and screenprint with halftone blocks. 732 x 583 mm. (28¾ x 23 in). Printed and published by the artist in an edition of 50.
The artist says, *'I was listening to a lot of Joan Baez and other 1960s songs and this connected with the idea of the other place, a spiritual home of some kind. I cut the pagoda out of The Times. I thought it was such a perfect shape to go with the circle ... something very peaceful'.*

Landranger by Carinna Parraman, 2000. Collagraph, screenprint and maps, cut into 50 mm (2 in.) squares, double-backed onto hessian. 1400 x 1000 mm (55⅛ x 39 in.). Printed and assembled by the artist. Unique work.

The artist says, '*My interests lie in the mapping of the landscape ... My work is fixed in a grid format. This modular method of working could be regarded as a constraint, but for me it is liberating ... the position (of the squares) in the grid is randomly determined ... Duchamp described this method of art production as "combating logical reality".*'

the image in the artist's mind needs the fineness of an etched line in some parts but also the covering power of screenprinted ink in others, then the combination of etching with screen is logical. Other common combinations are lithography with blind embossing, woodcut with linocut, lithography with screenprinting and relief with etching. Printing on a 3D-form – whether it is made from cast paper pulp, ceramic, resin or aluminium, for example – suggests the need to print on a transferable base sheet or to set up a screenprinting unit similar to those used to print bottles in industry. Printmakers are endlessly ingenious.

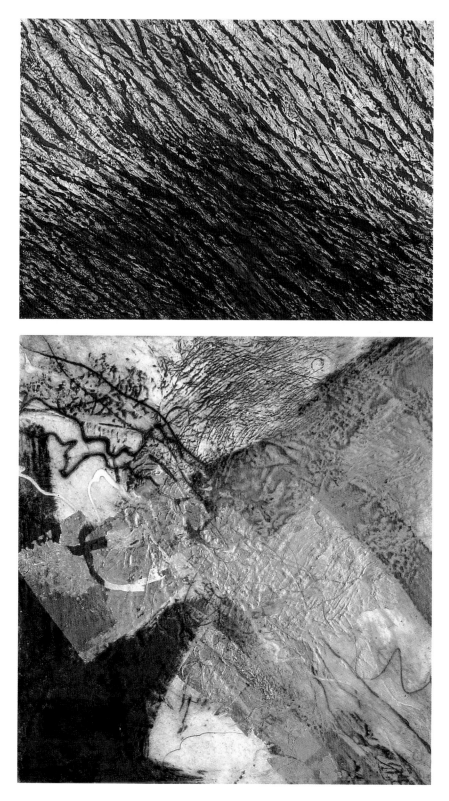

In the Beginning by Irene Scheinmann, 1998. Collagravure, 560 × 760mm (22 × 30 in). Printed and published by the artist from a card matrix made with carborundum and glue and printed in intaglio and relief.

Inferno I by Brenda Hartill RE, 2003. Intaglio, 490 × 460mm (19 ¼ × 18 ⅛ in). Printed and published by the artist in an edition of 100.

The artist says, '*The technique is collagraph made with embedded plant material, plaster, glue, Hammerite, varnish and carborundum on a zinc plate. It is printed once through the press with 'rubs' technique colouring different levels of the plate. The print is enriched with copper leaf. The plant material is used as the basis of the work to impart the energy of growth and life. Other marks are added to emphasise the dynamics of fire, creating an apocalyptic image, with copper leaf adding an element of heat and light.*'

Experimental prints are a very interesting category on their own. They are not intended to be editioned and are usually one-off prints. However, sometimes experimental proofing throws up the unexpected, and that image is then editioned.

Printmaking holds a very special place in the minds of non-printmaking artists, because it is possible to make a printing matrix by any of the traditional methods and then proof it in any number of colours, on any number of different coloured-paper backgrounds, and still keep your original matrix unchanged; if you modify a drawing or painting it is changed for ever. Imagine printing an etching in black ink on white paper and then in white ink on black paper: the effect will be quite different. The unique ability of printmaking to be used for experiment is recognised by artists whose main work is in other disciplines; they use it to refresh their ideas and to turn up unexpected solutions.

Spiral by Ingunn Eydal, 1986. Cast paper pulp and linocut, 95 x 88 mm. (3 ¾ x 3 ½ in). Printed and published by the artist in an edition of 60. The artist says, 'The spiral is made with paper pulp and glued onto the background. Both background and spiral are linocuts.'

Photography

During the early years of photography, in the mid-19th century, artists saw it less as an exciting additional tool than as a threat to their livelihoods. Eugène Delacroix (1798–1863), Édouard Manet (1832–1883) and many other artists made use of photography, but when it was widely adopted in commercial printing to produce cheaper and quicker illustrations they tried to dissociate themselves from the new medium. It became common to say that using photography in any way at all was cheating; art historians have shown, however, that artists such as Canaletto (1697–1768) used the camera obscura and camera lucida (forerunners of the modern camera) to help get the composition of a painting right, a practice that goes back at least as far as the mid-15th century. Photography is widely used today by artists to supplement the traditional sketchbook while gathering visual information.

After the Second World War, technical developments using photography in commercial printing coincided with a new movement in art which derived its inspiration from the cinema, advertising and press photographs. Screenprinting offered the greatest flexibility for the easy incorporation of photo-based images. Another advantage of the new method was its lack of a historical tradition, which might have inhibited artists seeking to create a new kind of print.

There has always been a current among pure photographers to elevate their medium to that of a fine art. One such attempt, first discovered in 1907, was called Bromoil. A silver-based photographic print on paper was bleached out by chemicals and replaced by oil-based inks or paint; these

Tapestry by Charlotte Hodes,
1999. Etching and aquatint, 340
x 290 mm (13 ⅜ x 11 ⅜ in).
Printed and published by the
artist in an edition of 10.
The artist says, '*This is one of a
series of four prints based on
Rubens's painting* Fortune *in the
Prado, Madrid. A photograph was
scanned into the computer and
manipulated through Photoshop
using filters. The dots were created
by using the vector-based program
Illustrator, giving smooth edges (as
opposed to the jagged edges
characteristic of the pixel-based
program Photoshop). The image
was then output onto transparent
film, being processed as a photo-
etching using a single copperplate.
The figure was printed intaglio
and the dots surface-rolled
[relief].*'

prints were shown in that state or sometimes transferred to another paper.
They were signed and issued in editions.

Photographs of all kinds are now offered for sale in signed limited
editions by reputable galleries. The negative is equivalent to the printing
matrix, from which many identical copies can be made. It is difficult to
argue that they are not prints, but are they artist's original prints?
Photography is usually seen as a quite separate category from printmaking;
it has its own exhibitions, criteria of appreciation and national collections.
Today, younger artists are using photography as the basis for highly original
work which goes beyond the mere mechanical recording of an image using
a camera. These artists, frequently working in the context of university
fine-art departments, are usually excluded from original print exhibitions,
though their work, printed as photographs, is really printmaking in the
creative and original sense.

The ambiguities in the word 'print' and the mixing of media by artists
today require the patron of visual arts to think rather deeply and to make
up their mind about what aspect particularly appeals to them.

Printing in Colour and Coloured Prints

The simple explanations already given of the traditional techniques describe the variety of marks which can be made in a single colour. When making a colour print it gets a whole lot more complicated.

One colour per printing matrix

The majority of colour prints use a separate block, plate, stone or screen for each colour, and they all have to be printed one on top of another in registration. Where the paper is used damp – as in intaglio, some Asian traditions and in relief printing on heavy papers – there is always a risk that the paper being dampened and dried between each application of a colour may not return precisely to the same dimensions as when the first colour was printed, and that subsequent colours may not be in registration. Most printing inks have to be allowed to dry between colours, but where paper stretch is a problem the answer is to print wet on wet. There are many different registration systems, including using marks or fixed pieces of card on the bed of the press; needles through the back of the paper sheet; windows the same size as the printing matrix cut in card or acrylic sheet; notches and pins and matching holes built into the press.

More than one colour per printing matrix

If areas of colour are quite distant from each other, it may be possible to ink up small parts with ink applied by a piece of felt or twist of padding in cloth, called a dolly or *poupée*. Small rollers can also be used, or ink applied

Orange Sun by Garrick Palmer RE, 1970. Lithographic colour proofs, 393 x 546 mm (15 ½ x 21 ½ in). Printed at the Curwen Studio and published by E.H. Newman.
The proofs are laid in series to show the progressive addition of colours. The right-hand bottom strip shows the first colour printed, a greenish black. The next strip shows the addition of the first colour on the sky. Subsequent proofs add green trees, red foreground, yellow, ochre, orange and purple; the top proof is the complete image.

by fingertip or brush or by cutting holes in a stencil to avoid getting ink in the wrong place. This is slow and careful work.

Viscosity colour printing from one plate

This method is only used for intaglio printing and relies on the fact that inks of different viscosities (stickiness) do not mix, so that inks can be applied in layers to the plate. Thick ink is rubbed into the most deeply etched or engraved parts, and the upper layers cleaned off. Then a medium sticky ink is delicately applied to the plate and again cleaned off the surface. Finally, a much more fluid ink can be rolled onto the surface of the plate, and the fully inked plate printed in one go. The ink on the surface will, of course, be the lower part of the printed image, with all the colours affecting each other depending on their degree of opacity or transparency.

Jigsaw colour prints

This method can be used to pull relief prints from woodblocks, plywood, lino, board, card, vinyl or other plastic sheets that are thin enough to be cut. Each area of colour can be separated, inked up in a different colour and the parts reassembled and printed as one. If the colours abut each other, cutting may leave a narrow line of unprinted paper between each area; this can be a feature of the design, or, if not wanted, each piece will have to be cut from a separate printing surface very accurately so that everything fits perfectly. If the main design is of one colour with only two or three extra patches of colour then holes can be cut in the block and small removable blocks cut to fit.

Reduction prints

This is an economical method for colour relief prints which can be adapted to lithography and screenprinting. It does need working out in the mind or on paper beforehand. Only one block is used. Any areas that should not

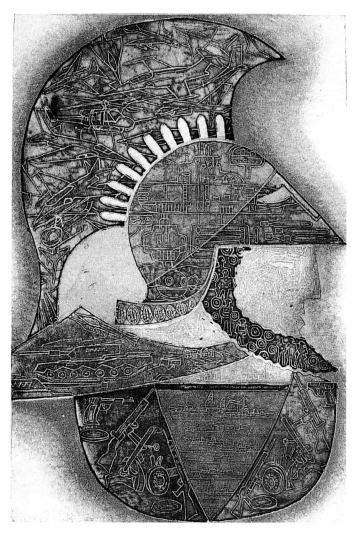

Ares by Cedric Green, 2002. Electrolytic etching on zinc, 250 × 160 mm (9⅞ × 6¼ in). Printed and published by the artist in an edition of 50. The artist says, 'This is an illustration plate in an artist's book called A Modern Atlantis … [I used] one plate with lines drawn through pencil carbon paper, stopped and deep-etched electrolytically in five steps, proofed in intaglio in black and overprinted in relief from the same plate in two colours.'

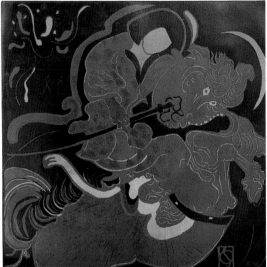

Warrior Woman – J.S. by Sheila Oliner, 1992. Reduction linocut, 460 x 445 mm (18 x 17 ¾in). Printed in four colours and published by the artist in an edition of six.

The artist says, *'This print was one of a series of paintings and prints loosely based on the Kuniyoshi prints. Also inspirational were the reduction prints of Picasso done in the 1950s. The "J.S." in the title was a dedication to my late friend Joanna Spence, feminist photographer, who was indeed a warrior woman.*

be printed at all (the unprinted paper can be treated as a colour in its own right) are cut out and the first colour printed – with an extra allowance for the complete edition for any mistakes that occur whilst the other colours are being printed. More of the block is cut away, and it is then printed in the second ink. This process continues until the last colour has been printed and there is hardly any of the block remaining. No wonder this method is also called 'elimination' or 'suicide printing'. It is not to be despised as a method: many of Picasso's very dramatic linocuts were done this way.

Using this method with lithography or screen requires the plate, stone or screen to be cleaned of part of the image just printed, or, alternatively, more work to be added.

Colour printing inks

Inks are made from pigments mixed with a binding agent to the consistency required for each method of printing. Pigments are derived from natural earths such as red ochre or simple elements such as carbon, the main ingredient of black ink. Ground-up minerals give more colours, but many others come from complex chemical processes. The price for each colour varies greatly: whereas the earth colours are cheapest, true ultramarine blue comes from lapis lazuli and is almost priceless; the ultramarine we use today is chemically produced and medium-priced. There can be colours which look the same but come from different sources. For example, Chinese white and titanium white are used for different effects. Some colours are naturally transparent and others opaque; if they overprint each other the effect will vary according to which is on top. There are also special fluorescent or metallic inks. Some pigments have a chemical reaction to copperplates, so avoiding action has to be taken by having the plate steel-faced. Some colours fade in bright light after a short time; look at advertising hoardings and see how the reds have faded over the months. However, artists always aim to use the best-quality colours so that their work will last.

Four-colour-process printing

This is the usual method of printing the colour photographic images which are seen in magazines, book illustrations, newspapers, brochures, leaflets and many reproductions. If you look at images from any of these sources under a magnifying glass, you will see various-sized dots in four colours: cyan (turquoise), magenta, yellow and black. These combine in your eye to give the impression of a full-colour photograph. The dots are called halftones and are created in a process camera in which a screen ruled with

Asparagus and Fish by Paul Croft, 1999. Lithograph, 290 x 220 mm (11³⁄₈ x 8⁵⁄₈ in). Printed and published by the artist in an edition of 12. The artist says that this is a *'five-run lithograph printed in yellow, red, blue and dark-green-black, and with chine collé as the fifth run. It also incorporates a Chinese chop mark of a fish printed by hand in red. The key drawing was on stone using crayon, tusche wash and ink-transfer technique (to create mesh, numbers and letters, etc). The yellow, red and blue were printed from positive photoplates – with additional tusche drawing.'*

black lines is placed before the image to be reproduced; filters are used to divide the image into four colours. The resulting four screened negatives can then be used to make the printing matrices for photo-relief, photo intaglio, photolitho or photoscreen, which will be printed in CMYK standard process colours.

The regular pattern of dots is easy to spot and used to be the simple way of recognising a reproduction, but some printers now use a random, or aquatint, screen, also called a 'stochastic' screen; this is more difficult to see and, with modern technology, the dots are smaller than ever. In traditional printing techniques the number of dots per inch will vary

Means of Escape (Alarm Clock) by Paul Coldwell, 2002. Four-colour offset lithography and lineblock relief print, 400 x 600 mm (15 3/4 x 23 5/8 in.). Printed and published by the Paupers Press.
The artist says, '*This image was one of a series of six under the title* Means of Escape, *the idea being that they would work both individually and as a sequence.*' The image was extensively worked on the computer in Photoshop from a photograph made by the artist. The image was printed by Mike Taylor at Paupers Press from digital files. The files enabled the dot layer to be separated and a line block to be made, which was then printed [relief] on top of the lithographic printing. This gives the effect of a slightly embossed surface where the dots are literally pressed into the surface.

according to the method used: fewer in screenprinting, most in lithography.

Four-colour-process printing is used by artists when they want to incorporate a photographic image, though they often modify it in some way or combine it with drawn elements.

Laser and ink-jet colour printing

Both techniques use a digital system which divides up the colours in the same way as the four-colour process. But the printing methods are different. The laser printer uses a laser beam to transfer an electrical charge onto a drum. The electrical charge then passes through a powdered pigment, which in turn is transferred to the substrate paper, where it is fused with heat; some machines first deposit the pigments onto an intermediary drum. Four passes are used, one for each of the colours (of CMYK) in turn. It is possible to see the pixel slab shapes of each colour with the naked eye. The ink-jet printer, on the other hand, sprays a variable amount of liquid ink through a nozzle onto the paper below; the dot pattern is more difficult to see without a magnifying glass. Initially, ink-jet printers used dye-based inks, which proved very fugitive; but today pigment-based inks are used by printmakers, and these have a much longer light-life.

Coloured prints

If a print has watercolour, pastel, crayon or any other colour added after printing, it cannot belong in a uniform edition, as each print is bound to be slightly different. Some artists have been exploring this form of hybrid print, and publishers rather like the idea as a print made in this way can be

Paris Beast III by Richard Anderton, 2003. Ink-jet print, 1040 x 1100 mm (41 x 43 ¼ in). Printed and published by the artist.
The artist says he *'developed a fascination with man's interpretation of animals … I have catalogued and captured the artisans' interpretations through photography rather than drawing, so that I do not detract from the essence and quality of their work… The ability to manipulate the design on the computer is part of a mystical method for setting free these creatures from their original environment.'*

sold as a unique work at a higher price. In some cases the workshop where the print was editioned also adds the hand-applied extra colour based on a sample done by the originating artist; of course, the end result does not have the artist's actual mark-making. This is an example of the abandonment of traditional practices, and it shows why the whole question of what constitutes an original print can seem so confusing.

The Sequence of Making a Print

Idea and matrix

A print starts out as an idea in the head of the artist which somehow has to be translated into the matrix or printing image. The development that the idea undergoes is conditioned by the operation of each printing method, since methods differ considerably, not least in the amount of changes or corrections that can be made. For example, a cut in wood cannot be undone, whereas a copperplate can withstand considerable reworking before the metal is weakened. The cost of materials is also a factor: a mistake in a lino block, a fairly cheap material, might persuade the artist to start again on a new block unless hours of very detailed cutting have already been done. Wood engraving blocks are expensive by comparison,

A group of different relief and intaglio matrices. From top left clockwise: incised rubber compound, aquatinted copperplate, photopolymer, heliorelief on wood, carborundum on acrylic, wood engraving on boxwood, process-engraved metal mounted on wood; and in the foreground left to right: woodcut, rubber stamp and another small process-engraved block.

and to some extent this is revealed in differences in technique: patient, controlled wood engraving, but much freer, less inhibited linocutting. Where the materials are expensive the artist puts in more preparatory planning by way of accurate measurements, reliable registration systems and the correct choice of ink and paper. Most of the time is taken up with the preparation of the printing matrix rather than the actual printing.

Some artists prefer to work out the design fully as a guide and even draw a plan for each colour. This is helpful in lithography, for example, where the third colour created by overprinting one colour on another can be difficult to visualise when drawing on the stone or plate in black litho ink or crayon (it is coloured black so that it can easily be seen) which will eventually be printed in yellow or blue.

Intaglio printmakers frequently start work on a plate without prior visual preparation of their idea. An early proof is taken so that the artist can see what the inked incisions look like; then they will plan further work. This is where experience counts: a certain depth of engraved line will print a certain way; a wash on a litho stone looks stronger than it will eventually print; a burnished area on a mezzotint plate may look shiny and smooth, but in reality there is still enough texture to hold some ink, and the result is greyish.

The general trend among practitioners is towards the conscious adoption of printmaking for its own special qualities as a medium of expression. The actual working of the matrix, in terms of metal, stone, wood, or whatever materials are used, is a very important element in the act of creating a print. There is far more involvement with the materials than with, for example, painting; some of those artists who were enchanted by what the computer can do are now realising that they are working at a distance from the end product, which can be dehumanising. For many artists, the struggle with the intransigence of some materials and the physical effort required are part of the satisfaction they experience when a good print is the result of long labour.

Proofing

Even with great experience it is not always possible to judge the effect of ink on paper in advance; so when the printing matrix seems ready it is time to proof the image. Mistakes can be seen and corrections made. Alternative papers and inks can be tried. A 'broken' black

The author printing from a plywood block on a cast-iron 1868 Albion press.

(a black ink with a little blue or some other colour added) may give a markedly better result than straight black. A change of paper can bring out a richness of detail only partially revealed by a standard proofing paper.

The order of printing colours is vital: yellow printed on top of black gives a green; printed underneath it will be obliterated. It is usual that the first colour to be proofed is the matrix with the most work, so that it acts as a guide for the subsequent colours; this helps to check that the registration system is working, though it may not be the final printing order. In a multiblock/plate/stone/screen composition, a proof in black of the first matrix can be transferred to the next blank matrix as a guide for drawing the next colour areas.

This is also the time to record the ingredients of a coloured ink and whether additives have been used to thin or thicken it, or to make it more transparent. When the time comes for editioning, the artist then knows the relative proportions when mixing enough ink for the whole print run. The amount of dampening the paper receives and the pressure to be used on the press both affect the printing; these are also worked out during proofing.

Alterations, corrections and re-proofing

A proof can sometimes be an outright failure: the artist's mental picture of the final image may not have been translated into the printing matrices, and considerable alterations or corrections may be required.

More cutting or engraving on relief and intaglio blocks or plates is relatively easy, but to reinstate an already worked area can be very difficult. Relief blocks can be filled with plastic wood but it is never really satisfactory; it is better to cut out a rectangle and insert a new piece. This is particularly difficult with wood-engraving blocks, which are quite thick, hence the very deliberate and controlled work wood engravers exhibit trying to avoid any mistakes. Metal plates can be burnished on the surface

Making Waves by Irene
Scheinmann, first state 2000,
second state 2003. Intaglio from
a carborundum and glue
matrix, 550 × 680 mm (21⅝ ×
26¾ in).
The artist says that the first
state was proofed in blue and
set aside. Then three years later
she cut 80 mm (⅛ in) off the
left-hand side and also
separated the top and bottom
halves. It was proofed again in
yellow and green on the top
and yellow and red on the
bottom with a space between
the halves. This space was filled
in by dilute ink by hand.

and then hammered on the back to raise the area ready again for new
work, this is where the malleability of copper is an advantage and why
intaglio is one of the most popular methods of printmaking. Photo-based
images cannot readily be altered once they have been processed onto the
printing matrix; it will usually be necessary to go back to the positive or
negative and remake the matrix.

Changes and corrections are usually re-proofed to check the result.
These proofs, known as 'states', can be of great interest as they show the
development of an image through an amount of trial and error intended to
strengthen or simplify it. These pulls are also called 'working', 'trial' or
'stage' proofs, and they are very collectable in their own right.

Paper for printmaking

Paper is an integral part of the print, and, though we tend to concentrate
on the image itself, the choice of paper is important. Artists work with
papers of all kinds and as such they are aware of the very variable
properties of this versatile material. It can have remarkable strength even
when wet; when oiled it becomes semi-transparent and was used in this
state for windows in place of glass in China and Japan. In the form of
paper pulp it can be moulded and in sheet form deeply embossed.

Paper is traditionally made from a pulp of cellulose fibres suspended in
water, which is allowed to settle in an even layer in a rectangular sievelike
frame called a 'mould'. It is turned out onto mats of felt to drain and dry.
Early Chinese sources say that the first paper was made from scraps of silk;
others claim old, rotten fishing nets were the first material used. Paper is
made of plant material from a variety of sources, such as cotton, linen,
grasses, reeds, tree bark, bamboo or sugar cane; whole trees are used to
make ordinary papers, but as they contain impurities which make them
turn brittle and discoloured they are not used by artists for high-quality
work. Good-quality old paper was made from carefully selected linen rags
and has lasted hundreds of years. The best-quality paper used by artists
today is made from new linen (flax), cotton and certain tree and shrub
barks. The addition of manila (hemp) gives strength; other fibres give
softness, hardness or transparency. Papyrus is not strictly a paper, though

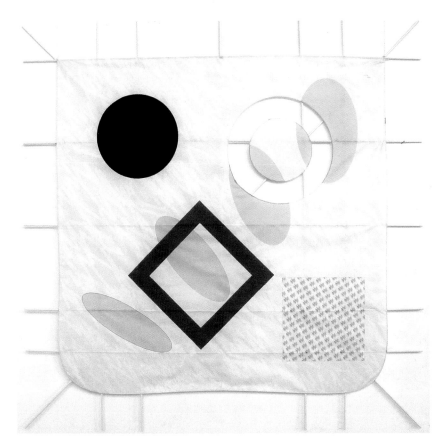

Golden Section Kite by Steve Hoskins RE, 2004. Screenprint on Japanese paper and glass fibre rods with traditional knots, 560 x 760 mm (22 x 30 in). Printed and published by the artist.

The artist says, '*Paying homage to traditional kite manufacture … these works are only possible due to a marriage of late 20th-century technology and the unsurpassed quality of a delicate sheet of handmade paper … The imagery used is often based on mathematical proportion and Euclidian geometry.*' The kite can be flown.

our own word derives from this beaten and layered pith of a sedge. Papyrus is still made today in Egypt and can be used for hand-printing.

The basic natural materials provide the various colours, textures and behaviours of the paper, which the artist takes into account when choosing the most suitable kind for each image. Artists have printed on other materials, such as vellum (the skin of a newborn calf), textile, metal and plastic, but paper has proved the most versatile and durable.

Whatever the source of the fibres in paper, the raw material is first softened, or retted, in water, then cleaned, and then beaten to a pulp in water to separate the fibres. To make handmade paper, the vat-man scoops just the right amount of pulp into the mould, then shakes it to distribute the fibres evenly and cause them to interlock whilst the water drains off. The delicate sheet is transferred to a wool felt, then another felt is placed on top, followed by another sheet of paper, then another felt, and so on – until the pile of papers and felts can be gently pressed so as to wring out all the water from the paper. The sheets are matured and dried slowly in airy lofts.

Papermaking is a trade with many traditions and much regard for the purity of the water supply as well as for the weather. One mill in Britain refused to make paper in August; the wind was always in the wrong direction! Many artists make their own paper expressly to be part of the

La Voisine by Sarah Bodman, 1999. Artist's book in the form of a sequence of images on different papers, printed by screen, etching and letterpress and presented in a box covered in printed and painted paper, 150 x 150 x 150 mm (6 x 6 x 6 in). Printed by the artist in an edition of three.

image. This was the case with David Hockney's Pool series, for which he directed buckets of coloured pulp to be poured to a specific pattern. Other artists make 3D formed paper sheets in irregular shapes on which they can print.

Making paper by hand is a slow process, and a mechanical method was invented in the early 19th century in which the vat-man's flat mould was replaced by a mesh cylinder which revolved in a vat, picking up pulp and depositing it in a continuous web to drain and be dried. This mould-made paper is widely used by printmakers, being made of the same pure material as handmade paper. The majority of everyday papers, such as newsprint, magazine and book papers, cartridge and writing papers, is made on a Fourdrinier machine, invented in 1807, in which the pulp is sprayed onto a porous web and quickly dried. Since about 1850, most mass-produced paper has been made from wood pulp and as such is not intended to last; thus the pages of books made in the last 150 years are fragile and tend to discolour.

Handmade papers are the strongest because the fibres are long and well interlocked; they are made of pure ingredients and are correspondingly expensive. Mould-made papers are not strong as handmade, the fibres being less well interlocked; but they are still made of good-quality materials and are also less expensive than handmade. Machine-made papers are not strong, being made of short-staple materials such as wood, which contains impurities; they will not last, but they do have the virtue of being cheap.

Textures and edges

Artist's papers are made with various surface textures: rough, NOT and hot-pressed. The natural drying of the fibres gives a rough surface on handmade paper; this is accentuated in the making of mould-made paper by using rough felts. Handmade NOT paper is pressed between boards to reduce the texture; mould-made machines use fine felts. Handmade paper is also hot-pressed between sheets of polished zinc, giving it a smooth surface; mould-made paper is similarly treated to make it very smooth. Machine-made papers are usually given textures by being calendered with smooth or textured rollers. 'Art' papers used for fine-quality reproductions in books have a surface of china clay; and many very-white-looking papers are coated with 'optical brighteners', which absorb ultraviolet rays and then emit them as blue light, thus increasing the apparent brightness – in the long term they lose this property and look dingy.

The most common finish to paper used by printmakers is gelatin or synthetic glue, which is either coated on the paper or is mixed into the pulp; this hardens the surface and strengthens the paper when dampened. Lithography and relief printing are generally printed on paper with little or no size, and intaglio on sized paper; screenprinting is very versatile, but sized papers are used when a smooth surface is required for fine detail or halftones.

The feathery edge around a sheet of handmade paper is called the deckle after the detachable frame used to contain the pulp in the mould, under which a little pulp inevitably seeps. The deckle varies according to the length of the fibres in the pulp. The natural deckle is imitated in mould-made paper by a rubber strap or water jet along the length of the paper; it only shows on the two short sides of the sheet, the long sides being torn when the sheet is detached from the web. Machine-made papers always have guillotined edges sharp enough to cut the skin. Some artists insist that the deckle is an integral part of the sheet, not only to prove the quality of the paper but also for its aesthetic value. Other artists prefer to cut off the deckle for either of two reasons: they may wish to deny the handmade character of the paper because it is at odds with the nature of the image, or, if the register is very tight in, say, four-colour halftone work, the edges must be at accurate right angles for the colours to synchronise on mechanised presses. If a deckle is present on a finished print it should not be cut off to fit a frame, or the value will be reduced.

17.04.02 – 5 by Michael Brick, undated. Screenprinted monotype, 400 x 400 mm (15 ¾ x 15 ¾ in). Printed by Kip Gresham and published by the Print Studio, Cambridge. This unique print is on a handmade Japanese paper and is printed right to the edge of the paper, thus emphasising the deckle. The contrast between the hard-edged image and the soft-edged paper is intentional and ought to be maintained when the print is framed.

Watermarks, stamps and chop marks

The watermark in a sheet of paper can be seen if it is held up to the light. The design is made out of wire and fixed to the mould mesh or cylinder; it leaves a thinner layer of pulp over the design. The watermark is usually the device of a paper-mill and is important in identifying papers and prints. Paper is sometimes made specially for a suite of prints and thus may incorporate a particular artist's signature or publisher's mark.

Blind embossed ciphers are frequently seen in one corner of the paper. They are another means of identification that does not visually affect the image. Most chop marks or embossing stamps are applied by publishers when the edition is ready for sale. Some artists also use a device similar to an Asian seal, which sometimes incorporates a phrase such as 'printed by the artist' or 'hand-printed'.

Editioning and cancelling

Once a definitive proof has been obtained it is marked 'passed for press', 'ready for printing' or '*bon à tirer*' (BAT), and signed by the artist to indicate approval; this proof is then the guide for printing the edition (see p79).

Slight variations in manual printing are inevitable and a welcome sign of the individuality of each print. Mechanised printing tends to be extremely accurate, but to insist on absolute exactitude in all the prints in an edition seems, to me, contrary to the spirit of printmaking. On the other hand, wide variations are not to be encouraged either, as they must reduce the intention expressed by the definitive proof and therefore by the artist.

If the printing is done in a professional workshop, the whole edition is printed in one go. Artists who print their own work might print only part of the edition and leave the rest till later. Printmaker's paper is very expensive and not everybody can afford to buy 50 or more sheets at once. There is also the boredom factor of printing the same image over and over, as well as the business of setting aside enough continuous time. However, artists do need to keep accurate records of the printing of part editions to ensure that the quality is maintained when the remaining portion is printed. At some stage in their career, an artist may need to show many different images rather than numerous copies of a carefully chosen few. Digital printmaking offers, for the first time, the possibility of printing on demand. This is very attractive for artists, because, though initially the making of the digital instructions takes a long time, there is an obvious saving in both time and money in needing to print a particular image only when an order comes in.

It used to be common when the edition had been printed to cancel the matrix so that no further copies could be pulled. Cancellation involved defacing the block or plate by scoring or cutting a cross or by drilling holes through the material. Chemicals were used to deface a lithoplate and stones were usually ground down and reused; the stencil was stripped off a screen. Sometimes a proof of the cancelled matrix was taken as evidence, and these too are now being collected as very unusual objects. Today, cancellation rarely occurs – it just seems to have gone out of fashion.

Checking, numbering and signing

After printing each impression is checked for defects. These might include a fault in the paper; a tiny dust particle not previously noticed, or a part of the image that did not print well; a colour that is under- or over-inked or

Opposite:
Finnegan's Lake by Gillian Ayres, 2001. Lift ground and aquatint with carborundum intaglio and hand-painting, 749 x 635 mm (29 ½ x 25 in). Published by the Alan Cristea Gallery in an edition of 35. Reproduced courtesy of Gillian Ayres and the Alan Cristea Gallery. Note that on the left beneath the image the letters B.A.T. and the artist's signature are written, indicating that this is a proof which has been passed for press (*bon à tirer*) and that the edition can now be printed.

slightly out of register with the other colours; incorrect positioning on the sheet; or a dirty thumb-mark.

Each print is then numbered in pencil, usually on the left below the image. Numbering is done in the form of a fraction: 20/75 indicates that it

Ken Kiff looking at a proof of
an aquatint at Studio Prints
workshop.

is number 20 in an edition of 75. The number, however, will not indicate
that it was printed first or 20th, because in a colour print the last sheet of
the first colour in a pile becomes the first to have the second colour added
and so on. Since very large editions can be printed without loss of quality
using lithography and screenprinting, the first or last prints will not show
any signs of wear or loss of detail. The number might be significant on a
single-colour drypoint, fine-line etching, aquatint or mezzotint, which can
wear, but today the plates are steel-faced to counter any possibility of this
happening.

The artist then signs each print in pencil, usually on the right just below
the image. Sometimes the artist will also add a title between the number
and signature. Pencil is used because if it is tampered with – for example,
replaced by the faked signature of a more famous artist – the fibres of the
paper will be disturbed and can be seen under a raked light or magnifying
glass. If pen and ink are used, it is difficult to tell apart from a printed
signature. Printed signatures are often seen on posters, unlimited editions
and reproductions; the term is 'signed on the plate', meaning that
individual prints have not been signed and approved by the artist.

The edition

The total number of prints intended for sale (or for distribution in the case
of a commemorative edition) comprises the numbered edition; this has to
be decided in advance. Occasionally, second editions have been taken of
very popular images in the past, particularly in wood engraving; it is not
considered good practice today, but, should it happen, 'second edition'
should be clearly written beside the number. The size of the edition will

affect its value; generally, editions over 150 are considered too large, though not in Europe, where they have been more common. Large editions are printed whenever there is a 'print boom' and demand exceeds supply. At present small editions are the norm; as few as 25 is common. Given modern printing techniques, most editions are artificially restricted.

Tower Bridge by Joseph Winkelman PPRE, 2002. Etching on copper, 300 x 640 mm (11¾ x 25³/₁₆ in). Printed and published by the artist in an edition of 150.

Artist's and other proofs

Over and above the edition copies there are a number of identical pulls of which the artist's proof is most commonly seen for sale. Artist's proofs are intended for the record or archive of the artist, but copies are often given away as gifts to family and friends; artists frequently swap proofs with friends. In place of the edition number is written 'artist's proof', shortened to 'AP'; '*épreuve d'artiste*' is shortened to '*EA*'. The convention is that these proofs should not exceed 10 per cent of the numbered edition. Sometimes working proofs are also named as artist's proofs; there is no real standard practice among artists.

If the edition has been printed in a professional editioning workshop, it is usual to give them one or two proofs for their own archive (the Tate Britain print collection is largely based on the gifts of workshop archives). Where several printers, editors, publishers and distributors are involved, which is not uncommon if artists in different countries contribute to a portfolio project, they may also be given a proof which is designated as '*hors commerce*', or 'HC', meaning it is not considered part of the edition for sale. Proofs with a line of dedication to a friend or charity sometimes appear in a sale and are of great interest to collectors because of their uniqueness.

The role of the publisher and printer

Both publishers and printers have played an important part in the development of modern prints. They have worked in partnership with artists and together shared and solved many problems, both technical and aesthetic, and they have given artists opportunities to explore the wealth of resources that printmaking offers.

The art dealer and publisher Ambroise Vollard (1865–1939) was a particularly important figure. Between 1900 and his death, he encouraged many artists to make prints. Most of his publications assumed the form of elegant and sumptuous illustrated books. The first book, published in 1900, was *Parallèlement* by Paul Verlaine (1844–1896) with lithographs by Pierre Bonnard (1867–1947). Vollard also commissioned Picasso, Chagall, André Derain (1880–1954) and many others to produce remarkable books in which the choice of poet, typography, artist and method of printmaking are all finely judged. Other important publishers at that time were Maeght and Kahnweiler in Paris and Skira in Switzerland, but almost every cultural centre in Europe boasted its own publishers of *éditions de luxe*. These publishers acted as catalysts, matching artists with printers and often financing the whole process as well as cultivating a list of wealthy subscribers to support each demanding project.

More recently, a number of distinguished publishers, hoping for both profit and glory combined with their genuine love of art and a desire to make fine printmaking more accessible, have moved away from the format of the rare illustrated book towards single prints, or sometimes suites of prints from which some would be sold individually. America became the postwar focus. The best-known publishers, who also maintained their own workshops and sought to be very hands-on, were Tatyana Grosman's Universal Limited Art Editions and Ken Tyler's Gemini Graphic Editions Limited – there are now many more producing exciting work all over North America. In Britain there has been equally important support from publishers such as Editions Alecto and Curwen Prints, and prestigious galleries such as Marlborough Fine Art. It is interesting to note that a number of key people, such as Chris Prater of the Kelpra Studio in Britain and Ken Tyler in the States, started out as commercial printers, whereas Stanley Jones of Curwen Prints and Kip Gresham of Gresham Studio were trained first and foremost as artists; the former tended to be keener on innovation in technique and the latter more sympathetic to the aesthetic solutions. Whatever their backgrounds, these master printers have been responsible for the most remarkable flowering of late 20th-century art.

The relationship between the artist and printer is the making or breaking of a good print. If their temperaments are compatible, the printer will anticipate what the artist wants to do, suggest ways of doing it, invent solutions and generally contribute an enormous amount to the work published. In the case of each of those mentioned, the work would have been inconceivable without the printer and is the result of intense and close collaboration: few artists can keep up with the technological

Deptford II by Albert Irvin, 2000. Screenprint with woodblock. Printed and published by Advanced Graphics London in an edition of 125.

Advanced Graphics say that *'Albert Irvin and Anthony Frost work onto draft film (textured plastic sheet) to make their shapes and elements, using just black ink in the studio. The elements are made into screens by the technicians in the studio, in some cases after being broken down by a light box, to expose the shapes to more or less light, so that when they are rebuilt at the printing stage they have the feel of brush strokes.*

'The elements are then placed together at proofing stage, when decisions about colour and location are made. Each individual element is printed by the technician at the artist's direction and notes are taken so that the composition can be replicated at the editioning stage.

'If the artist requires woodblocks to be integrated into the process (to add texture and weight of colour) the blocks are cut by hand before being inked with a roller or brush.

'Each artist will decide when the proofing stage is complete, usually at 30 to 60 printings.'

developments of today, and only specialist printers know the full range of inks, papers and finishes.

An example of happy collaboration is the series of etchings *The Artist and his Model* which Picasso produced during the seven months from March to October in 1968. The brothers Aldo and Pierre Crommelynck set up a press near Picasso's villa in the South of France. They kept him constantly supplied with prepared plates, and whilst he was drawing they were biting and proofing the plates drawn on the day before. Three hundred and forty-seven intaglio prints of great inventiveness resulted.

Another fruitful alliance was that between Henry Moore and Stanley Jones of the Curwen Studio. Jones made a point of producing a wide range of subtle colour variations while proofing Moore's lithographs. He also proofed one image on top of another or turned one upside down. These experiments delighted Moore and were frequently chosen for editioning. Such creative master printers are often underrated, though of course the ideas still come from the artist and the printers, in a sense, only serve to extend the artist's intention.

Framing and Conservation of Prints

The care of prints

It has been noticeable in the last few years that art galleries and museums have dramatically lowered the light levels where works on paper are exhibited. Scientific investigation has revealed that paper and textiles are particularly vulnerable to the conditions of modern life: atmospheric pollution, bright lights and central heating.

Light is a prime suspect in the deterioration of paper, affecting it progressively and irreversibly, and gradually provoking a chemical reaction that turns even the best of papers brittle and discoloured. Light also makes most colours fade, whether painted or printed. Colours vary in their susceptibility and diluted colours are more fugitive than well-pigmented ones. This can be easily demonstrated in everyday life if you look at a year-old newspaper or a billboard after six months' summer sun. Artists have always taken a keen interest in different papers and are well aware of the detrimental effect of sunlight, but knowledge of artists' materials is now rarely taught in art colleges. In recent years, art suppliers have been replacing reliable traditional materials with synthetic ones, and they are cagey about divulging how these new materials are made.

The light rays at the ultraviolet end of the spectrum are the most damaging. Prints should never be hung in direct sunlight. Fluorescent tube lighting emits a considerable amount of ultraviolet light, whereas incandescent or tungsten bulbs, still the commonest form of domestic lighting, are safest of all. It is a question of degree: strong light induces damage more quickly; weak light takes longer.

Heat has two damaging effects: it dries out the natural moisture content of materials such as paper and wood and indoors it tends to create rising draughts of air which carry dust and polluted air into framed pictures, where it becomes trapped. Damp is equally dangerous, as it will cause the growth of mould, reveal any impurities in the paper (which cause the brownish marks known as 'foxing') and will eventually rot the paper. Damp walls are one hazard, but humidity can be as bad: if it exceeds 70 per cent or goes below 30 per cent the paper will be at risk. Also, insects that are partial to eating paper and pigments tend to flourish in areas of high humidity. I remember coating a sheet of paper with black poster paint and laying it on the floor one evening when I was in India; by morning there were interesting conceptual-art trails all over it, made by cockroaches who ate the paint.

Apart from natural hazards, prints can be damaged by bad framing: either using acidic backing, mounting boards and glues which can harm a work of art, or by not sealing the back well. In their enthusiasm for new materials artists sometimes give insufficient thought to their long-term behaviour. Prints incorporating collaged elements are giving museum curators many headaches, as these elements may react with each other; adhesives are major culprits, and I am sure everyone now avoids cellulose, masking and pressure-sensitive tapes as well as spray mounts. The rule with any work of art is that whatever is used must be reversible and non-damaging.

Museum conservators have said that, ideally, works on paper should be stored away from light and kept in an air-conditioned, temperature-controlled environment. All materials in contact with the paper should be acid-free, and there should be no points of pressure or restriction to the natural movement of the paper. Of course, conservators have a special duty of care since they keep the works of art for the benefit of the public and

Remember Me by Carmen Gracia RE, 2003. Etching, 80 x 80 mm (3 $\frac{1}{8}$ x 3 $\frac{1}{8}$ in). Printed and published by the artist. This print was also published as part of the RE Big Print, 2004. Framed with a plain silver moulding 12 mm ($\frac{1}{2}$ in) wide, and a window mount the same colour as the printed paper.

scholars. However, most of us do not live under museum conditions, and collectors have to do the best they can, particularly if they intend to keep works as family heirlooms, sell them at a profit or give them to a local or national collection. Collectors who plan that their acquisitions will eventually be placed in a museum have the same responsibility as a curator.

The basic rules for print conservation are:

1. Do not hang a print where it will catch direct sunlight.
2. Do not hang a print over a heater, radiator or hot-air duct.
3. Do not fix a light immediately over or close to a print.
4. Do not attach a print to any other material by irreversible means.

Framing

Framing is intended to protect as well as to display the work to its best advantage. There are three basic types of framing:

1. Framing according to the highest conservation standards, which is always going to be expensive;

2. Sensible framing that gives reasonable protection but cannot be considered permanent and should be reviewed every ten years; and
3. Temporary framing that gives little protection and should not really be used except for ephemeral works such as posters and reproductions.

Conservation framing

A frame to conservation standards is made up of a number of layers: glazing, mount, work of art, backing board, barrier, frame backboard, moulding and the fixing and sealing of the moulding to the backboard.

Glazing material should be good-quality picture glass, without defects or acrylic substitutes, which can be treated with a coating to exclude many of the harmful ultraviolet rays. Non-reflective glass has a slight texture, which breaks up glare but only really works when viewed from one direction; also, the print has to be in direct contact with the glass, which is not recommended.

The mount or mat is used to keep the print away from direct contact with the glass, which allows some natural movement of the paper and visually isolates the image from the frame. The mount is cut from acid-free conservation board with a neutral pH of 7 and with a window large enough to show the signature and number. The print is not attached to the mount but to the backing board, which is made of the same conservation board. The print is held in place with two or more hinges (depending on size) made from a pure long-fibred paper such as a Japanese paper, and should be glued with a reversible acid-free starch paste.

It is recommended that an inert barrier sheet, made of polyethylene terephthalate (Melinex® in Britain, Mylar® in USA), should be placed between the backing board of the print and the frame back, to prevent the migration of noxious substances from the backing and air.

As neither comes into contact with the print, the choice of either a wood or metal moulding is largely an aesthetic one: its role is to isolate the work of art visually from its surroundings so that it can be properly appreciated. The range of mouldings is very large both in size and colour as well as detail; a good framer will give you sound advice. Wooden mouldings can be plain, painted or gilded with real or artificial foil, and metal mouldings can be shiny, matt or painted. Boxes can be made for 3D works, using wood sides or moulded from acrylic.

The sealing of the back of a frame with a linen, paper or plastic tape to exclude dust is not supported by all conservators: some advocate placing a narrow strip of cotton felt in the gap between back sheet and moulding, thus letting in some air to allow for the print's natural movement but excluding dirt. Small metal pins or triangular darts keep the contents within the confines of the moulding.

Where prints which have no margins and the work goes right to the edge of the paper, or where a feature is made of the deckle and a window mount is inappropriate, the print can be hinged onto the backing board, with a thin spacer of acrylic or conservation board placed at the sides to keep the glass off the surface of the print. Conservation boards can now be found in a variety of colours, but, if a special effect is required using a

Trafalgar Square II by Ceri Richards, 1962. Lithograph, 585 x 812 mm (23 x 32 in). Printed and published by Curwen Prints Ltd in an edition of 70. Here it is given a simple wooden ramin frame and a window mount of neutral pH board the same colour as the printed paper.

non-conservation paper, it can be glued onto recommended board using acid-free paste. Coloured or metallised edges to the bevel-cut edge of the window mount are not encouraged, as the materials will come into contact with the paper of the print.

Sensible framing

This sort of framing can be far less elaborate if the collector is aware of certain hazards. A sensible frame will be made up of glazing, mount, print, backing board, frame back and moulding. It is worth insisting on good-quality picture glass if only to avoid surface distortion; ordinary-quality acrylic sheet is acceptable, but it does scratch. If no window mount or spacers are used, condensation inside the glass could be a hazard in some climates. Cheaper mounting boards are not acid-free like conservation board, and will eventually affect the print. A telltale sign is the turning orange of the cut edge of the window mount, indicating a high acid level; if this happens, the print should be removed.

Fixing the print in the right place is important. Prints should never be heat-mounted, glued down or fixed all round the edge: even if the glues are safe, which most are not, the paper will not breathe naturally and will sag or crack. Pressure pads put between the print and backing are not recommended, as this entails pressing the face of the print against the glass. A sheet of acid-free paper placed behind the print instead of expensive conservation board will give some protection. The old-fashioned backing board made of thin plywood or wood fibreboard is more dangerous than any paper-based card or boards. The gap at the back between moulding and backboard should be sealed with gum strip, though bear in mind that the gum is acidic; plastic parcel tape has only a short life.

Temporary framing

Short-term framing varies from a sandwich of glass and backing held together by clips to lengths of plastic or metal mouldings held together by hidden corner pieces. The disadvantage is that the print is held in contact with the glass and the backing board, and dirt can easily get in the sides and back. Cheap photographic-type frames are the same. Furthermore, the materials used will not be acid-free.

Not all framers are experienced in handling prints, so it is essential to make sure they carry out your instructions. The essential rules are:

• Never cut the paper of the print as it could reduce its market value and it is contrary to the intentions of the artists who has carefully chosen the position of the print and its margins
• Never fix the print with any tape or glue other than acid-free paste or tape
• Never heat-mount a print onto board or heat-seal the surface with plastic film
• Handle the sheet of paper with care, picking it up with both hands one on each side of the sheet. Paper creases and kinks if not held properly and such marks are impossible to completely eradicate.

DIY framing should be considered if the collector has the necessary skills, because all the conservation materials are now available by mail order, including mouldings with mitres cut to order.

Other ways of conserving prints

Conservators hold that prints should ideally be kept in a dark, dry place with the temperature controlled. Curiously enough, in the 18th and 19th centuries this is almost exactly what was done in the libraries of large town and country houses in which were housed books, maps and prints. Bookshelves around the walls provided excellent insulation from the excesses of heat and cold. In the centre of the room would be found a large print stand, which allowed plenty of space on top to open large portfolios and study the contents, and housed flat portfolios on wide shelves underneath. New acquisitions were shown to friends and family and knowledgeably discussed. Many collectors subscribed to the publication of suites of prints, which were issued in instalments, often at six-monthly intervals, and eagerly awaited. White-cotton gloves were kept for a guest who might arrive without a pair, though gloves were commonly worn at social occasions indoors. Thus prints were protected from the acid oils from fingertips that eventually leave marks on the paper. The antithesis of this sort of careful collecting was also manifest in the 18th century, when it became fashionable to decorate a print room by deliberately gluing prints onto the walls; special engraved borders and ribbons were printed to simulate a frame and its hanging.

The tradition of handling prints could well be revived in the home today, given a plentiful supply of white-cotton gloves. A work of art hanging on the wall tends to be ignored after a time, becoming simply a part of the furnishings; perhaps if it was seen only occasionally it would

keep its visual freshness and physical condition.

Portfolios are the common way of protecting prints. They are made of two flat boards hinged together with linen or some other tough fabric, and have three flaps to keep the contents from falling out. They come in various sizes traditionally based on handmade paper sizes such as imperial, royal and antiquarian (see Glossary). The portfolios available from art-supply shops will not be made of acid-free boards, so an interior barrier of acid-free paper or inert plastic should be added to protect the prints.

Special suites of prints are often presented in portfolios designed for the purpose by the artist or publisher. These portfolios are frequently made of exotic materials such as silk, velvet, leather, vellum, rare woods and metal sheets, and inlaid, embossed, printed and collaged with other materials comparable to the best of modern bookbindings. More conventional portfolios are covered with bookbinder's cloth and have the suite title and artist's name blocked on the front. Portfolios made by bookbinders cannot be relied upon to be made of safe materials.

Solander boxes, which rarely exceed 38 x 51 cm (15 x 20 in), are used for small prints. They have rigid sides usually about 8 cm (3 in) deep, and the hinged lid opens out so that the prints or drawings in one half can be

Dwelling Places by Helena Markson, 2000. Aquatint, 285 x 240 mm (11¼ x 9⅜ in). In boxed folios of ten prints – No. 7, *Succah*, shown here. Printed and published by the artist in an edition of five.

The Print Room at Blickling Hall, Norfolk, UK. An 18th-century solution to displaying prints: each print is pasted directly on the wall with a printed border around to simulate a frame and hanging bow above.
There are 52 prints in this room. This suggests that the owner is so wealthy that the conservation of the prints themselves is of little importance; but it also confirms the number of prints widely available at this time.
Reproduced by kind permission of The National Trust.

slid out with the minimum of handling. They are in general used by museums for print storage, where each item is protected by a window mount and backing board using conservation materials. A transparent sheet of inert plastic is sometimes put behind the window to ensure that the work is never touched by unprotected fingers.

Large books or albums of blank sheets of paper on which prints could be mounted were another traditional way of keeping works on paper. Contemporary prints tend to be too large to keep this way, but the method could be revived as a way of keeping small prints as long as the books were made of acid-free paper and the correct glue and hinges were used.

Artists also use plan chests with large shallow drawers, such as are made for architects; they can also be handsome pieces of furniture. The hazards of lifting large sheets of paper in and out of plan chests can be avoided by using large sheets of conservation board between groups of prints. The boards can also be simply hinged to keep prints in manageable sets. Finally, prints should be interleaved with acid-free tissue or paper, because some printing inks dry exceedingly slowly.

Damaged prints

Prints that suffer damage from overexposure to light, which discolours paper and makes colours fade, cannot be revived. Tears, creases and kinks in the paper can sometimes be repaired or at least diminished, but it requires a fully trained paper conservator to know the right methods and materials and how they should be used; this can be costly. The same goes for stains, such as foxing and water stains. Bad studio practice can leave thumbprints and smears of ink in the margins, which are only treatable with great care. First, try a soft putty rubber to lift off any loose material; if it is more persistent use the finest-grain sandpaper, but be aware that in doing so you are removing some of the paper fibres and you must smooth the area down again. If these tricks do not work, accept the fact that the value of the print is diminished. Paper conservation is a recognised university course in most countries, and conservators have their own professional bodies to uphold standards and to help the public find a suitable practitioner.

Transport of prints

Prints and drawings are probably the easiest works of art to transport, but there are certain methods to be recommended. Prints are most frequently packed in tubes, so it is most important that these are of sufficient strength: cardboard tubes should be not less than 4 mm (⅛ in) thick, and plastic tubes are stronger. It is equally important that the diameter should be large enough – a minimum of 8 cm (3 in) and preferably more – that the print is not rolled too tightly. To protect the ends of the print the tube should be at least 5–8 cm (2–3 in) longer top and bottom.

The print should be placed face up on a sheet of acid-free tissue with another placed on top. These sheets should then be rolled so that the roll is just less then the internal diameter of the tube, and then wrapped in another piece of tissue to keep the print rolled up and to protect it from rubbing against the inside of the tube. Pads of crumpled tissue put inside the tube at the top and bottom will stop it moving about in transit. Some tubes have push-on or screw caps; if not, round pieces of card should be cut and taped in place over the ends.

Most prints are rolled image inwards, but screenprints or any with a heavy ink load should be rolled image out (like a painting on canvas) so that should any fine cracks appear they will close up when flattened.

To remove a print from its tube should be easy if it is properly wrapped; but if the paper has splayed out use two clean fingers to grasp the innermost top corner of the print and twist towards the centre to tighten the roll – it should then come out safely. Having been removed, the print should be placed upside down on a clean flat surface and be given time to relax back into its former flattened state.

Some prints cannot be rolled and have to be transported flat between boards. These would include heavily embossed or collaged prints, or those with a very heavy ink load.

SECTION THREE

The Affordable Art Fair is now a very popular event. It started in London but now it also travels to other major cities. The works are priced at £3,000 and under, and galleries and groups of artists have informal stalls backed up by efficient sales and packing staff; works can be taken home immediately. The atmosphere is relaxed and informal and sometimes there are printmaking demonstrations; there is always a direct, open and friendly exchange between artists and public.

Where to Find Artist's Original Prints

Museums and libraries

The would-be original-print collector will find that museums are particularly valuable: many house important collections of historical prints; some aim to add contemporary prints to keep up to date with current trends; and some have displays explaining techniques. These collections show the gradual unravelling of the historical development of printmaking, and set standards for quality. Many of the collections are open by appointment only and are used mainly by art historians and researchers. So any visitors should decide in advance which specific work or works by a particular artist they would like to see; the staff are always very helpful. Items from the print collection, usually on a theme or focussed on an individual or school, are also often displayed in exhibitions open to the public. In addition, national museums have a policy of creating touring exhibitions, which go on loan to provincial museums that have the necessary high standards of light, humidity and heat control, as well as staff surveillance. A few museum shops sell artist's original prints as well as the ubiquitous reproduction.

Opposite
Wave and Flower by Ken Kiff, 1993. Soft ground and aquatint intaglio print, 405 x 250 mm (16 x 9⅞ in.). Printed at Studio Prints from three plates and published by Marlborough Graphics in an edition of 35. Copyright with the estate of Ken Kiff and reproduced by kind permission of Marlborough Graphics.

The Curwen Gallery, London in 1965, with its opening exhibition of lithographs, by, left to right, Alan Davie, Henry Moore and Robert Adams, printed and published by Curwen Prints Ltd. The gallery director, Rosemary Simmons, is talking to the printmaker Peter Daglish, who was due to have the next exhibition.

Many countries have important national libraries that include artist's original prints in their collections. The Bibliothèque Nationale in Paris has been collecting prints since the 17th century under its *dépôt légal* system, whereby one copy of anything printed must be given to the State (originally, it was a policy designed to prevent sedition). These institutions also exhibit parts of their collections and give access to scholars and interested members of the public.

Galleries and dealers

Some galleries and dealers specialise in artist's original prints. They tend to keep a large stock to give a wide choice of style and price range, and they are usually very knowledgeable. Galleries exhibit new editions, and give one-person shows and group exhibitions, whereas dealers tend to sell by appointment, often from their offices or homes. Both galleries and dealers may also publish editions and buy and sell at auctions. Galleries tend to develop close relations with their stable of artists and to promote them over a number of years, with the result that they are known for a certain type of work. One gallery may specialise in large abstract prints suitable for public spaces; another in smaller, domestic prints. Some galleries concentrate on a certain medium – for example, wood engravings seem to attract a very specific public – and so they build up a list of interested clientele for whom they will also seek out particular images. Some galleries are the retail outlet for a print workshop and thus may concentrate only on editions they publish; many societies of printmakers maintain a gallery to show their members' work. These galleries and dealers tend to be associated with the centre of large cities; sometimes they seem a little daunting to enter, but do not be intimidated, for it is in these galleries that you will see the most interesting work.

There are many smaller galleries to be found in suburbs, towns and villages, and these tend to be more friendly. They probably will not specialise in artist's original prints, but they may also sell paintings, sculpture, ceramics, glass and other crafts; they are less likely to be very knowledgeable about prints since they cover so many fields. They often cater to middlebrow tastes and support local artists; they are an excellent place to start looking at and buying prints. Ask to be put on their mailing lists, and go to private views of their exhibitions; you'll get a chance to meet the artists and ask them face to face about their work – most artists are delighted to tell you more about their aims and methods.

Shops and stores

A gallery within a store is now very common, particularly in America and Japan. These galleries may be run by the store, but more commonly they are branches of wholly separate galleries with premises elsewhere. Stores by their very nature cater for a wide cross section of the public, so the prints they stock are of general appeal; you are unlikely to see the latest avant-garde idea here.

Greenwich Printmakers' Gallery, London is owned and run by its artist members. It has a wide range of original prints at moderate prices and is a friendly and welcoming gallery.

Prints used to be sold in bookshops because the publishers often produced both books and prints, but that is very uncommon now. You will, however, see many artist's original prints in framing shops, usually mixed up with reproductions. This mixing up of chalk with cheese is one of the prime causes of confusion for the public. Perhaps the shops are hoping to enhance the value of reproductions, which are produced in large quantities and are mere mechanical copies of pre-existing images. These shops are primarily interested in selling framing, and as such they are very rarely knowledgeable or even concerned about the finer points of the argument over what constitutes an artist's original print.

Art fairs

One interesting facet of modern life has been the growth of national and international art fairs. These events used to be like trade fairs for publishers and dealers, but the public insisted on visiting them too and so they have grown, some to huge proportions. They are a wonderful opportunity to see many publishers and galleries under one roof and to be able to compare their artists – and prices. These organisations are rarely devoted only to printmaking, with the advantage that you will see the work of printmakers in the context of painting, sculpture and all the other media used by artists today.

There is also a trend towards similar gatherings with the particular aim of selling inexpensive art directly to the public. Here you will find individual artists exhibiting alongside print societies and galleries – again, a good opportunity to browse at your ease and most likely get a bargain.

Arts centres and colleges

Prints are frequently seen within an arts centre which may itself house printmaking studios and offer tuition. Art colleges and art departments within a university are the principal resources for the teaching of all forms of printmaking. The full-time courses lead to a degree and are specialised, but the institution may also offer evening or part-time courses to beginners and to artists wanting refresher courses. They all have end-of-year or graduation exhibitions, and these are excellent sources for lively young exciting art at reasonable prices. There is always the thrill of spotting the next star or seeing the beginning of a trend – and they are always fun to visit to soak up the atmosphere of palpable optimism. A student print may not be a good long-term investment, but then again it might be; whether it is or not, you will have the added satisfaction of giving encouragement at a crucial time. Some students want to charge unreasonably high prices: in their arrogance they see their work as comparable to the best in the land. They are unlikely to have any track record, so negotiate with them: most would prefer any sale to none.

Art departments also exhibit their own tutors' work, which is seen as the equivalent of the academic publishing required by research programmes. These shows are often of great interest: teachers of printmaking are

Ring by Mark Balakjian HonRE, 1997. Mezzotint, 95 x 80 mm (3 ¾ x 3 ⅛ in). Printed and published by the artist in an edition of 20.

frequently the leaders in exploring new ideas; they are also the defenders of printmaking traditions.

Open studios

Many towns hold days, even a week, of open studios to run concurrently with a local festival. They are widely advertised locally, offering the opportunity to visit a working studio to see how an artist, or a group of artists, has organised their workplace. Most artists are also willing to talk about their work. Some may give demonstrations as well as exhibiting work, which is usually at lower than gallery prices. You may see working sketches and proofs all leading to the finished image, which will give you an insight into an artist's ideas and the ways they develop these ideas. You will also begin to understand all the subtle decisions the artist has to make as the concept is gradually transmitted first to the printing matrix or matrices and then to the choice of paper, the proofing and printing.

Buying and Selling

Direct buying

Prints exist mainly in editions, but many galleries also show single, unique versions called monoprints (see Glossary) or monotypes. With editioned work there may be two prices – one for the framed work hanging on the wall and also an unframed price for another print from the same edition – or the framed print may be the only copy they have, which is for sale as framed, complete. The gallery may offer a framing service for any unframed prints they have, or, if not, the buyer can take it away in a tube and find their own framer.

Frequently you see a framed print hanging on the gallery wall, and having decided to buy you are disconcerted to be offered another one from a plan-chest drawer. Today's very high standard of printing means that the prints will be almost identical all through the edition, allowing for minor differences if the work is hand-printed. Nobody will mind if you scrutinise the one you are being offered.

Doubt about whether a print is the right one for a special position or whether the recipient, if it is a gift, will like it as much as you do can be resolved by asking if you can take the print on approval. Most galleries will allow this, though they will also need a substantial deposit and may put it in a temporary frame. A gallery will frequently secure the sale of a large number of prints to a company, university or similar body, something that will probably need committee approval, by taking the trouble to show the committee a portfolio of prints, or these days more likely slides or a CD-ROM.

The right time to ask for any information which has not been freely offered about an artist or print is before you buy. Any reluctance on the part of the gallery, or lack of detailed knowledge, should be viewed with concern. Most countries have strict consumer-protection laws governing accuracy of information, but the very looseness of some terms in printmaking leaves these laws open to abuse.

It is also worth asking a gallery what is their policy on returns or exchanges. Some galleries want to encourage collectors and realise that their customers' tastes may change over time; as they want to build a loyal client base, they will most likely be flexible about exchanges. For this reason, it is even more important to keep the print in good condition.

Buying at auction

This can be fun, and scary too. There is usually a viewing day prior to the sale, and the more prestigious auction houses will also issue an illustrated catalogue. They often give a suggested price, which gives you some idea whether the print is likely to be within your range. A reserve price is given when the owner will withdraw the print if it does not reach that minimum level. Many auctions will take your name and give you a number, which, should you be successful, you will show to the auctioneer when the sale is

Kelston Fine Arts in Bath, UK is a gallery within the home of Mrs Susan Howell. Twice a year she opens her house by invitation and shows a changing collection of prints and small paintings. She spent many years specialising in selling prints to corporate buyers in large office complexes; now her clients are looking for domestic-size works and they welcome seeing work on the walls of a real home.

concluded. Bidding is usually indicated by raising a hand or number, or making some such gesture. The auctioneer may also have staff near him taking telephone bids from interested parties not present. When the sale is done you must be prepared to pay on the spot. You then arrange transport or collection of your purchase. In some cases you will also pay a buyer's premium on top of the purchase price.

Bargains can sometimes be had at auctions, but remember that the people bidding against you will probably be dealers with a pretty shrewd idea of the real value of a given work. They may be buying for a customer who tells them a ceiling price beyond which they must not go; they may be buying for a museum, a gallery or to build up enough works for a specific exhibition.

It is advisable to go to a number of auctions just to watch and listen. At the major auction houses you will start recognising regulars and get an idea of their areas of interest. It is an amusing and educational pastime just to be there.

Indirect buying

The collector who does not have the opportunity to visit galleries and auctions regularly should consider buying by mail order or on the Internet. Reputable galleries and publishers offer catalogues with a wide range of prints at reasonable prices. They will not be outrageous, controversial or avant-garde, but they are nevertheless a good way to start collecting. Prints will usually be dispatched in tubes, with the option of returning them in good order if you are unhappy with them, as with any other mail-order sale.

The undoubted disadvantage of this remote way of buying is that small reproductions in catalogues rarely do justice to the work. The quality of the paper on which the image is printed and the tactile surface of it cannot

Pandora I by Albert Irvin, 1999. Screenprint with woodblock, 840 x 685 mm (33 x 27 in). Printed and published by Advanced Graphics London in an edition of 125.

be conveyed. The colours are often distorted and the compression of scale can under- or overemphasise some aspects. If you know the print already then there is no problem; if you don't, the work you receive may be a disappointment.

There have been, from time to time, cowboy mail-order print offers which, if not dishonest, come very close to it. The information they give is often misleading and should be treated with caution. These offers specialise in ambiguous descriptions the main aim of which is to sell a low-value item, usually a reproduction, for a high value by implying that it is an artist's original print. Offers which promise to be an investment for the future are best avoided – nobody can truthfully make that claim.

Prints by artists who are now dead, particularly if the prices are low but the artist is famous, are probably restrikes (see Glossary) or may be clever reproductions designed to deceive – the *giclée* print strikes again! In general it is better to stick to companies with a good name, who have been dealing long enough to have proved their genuine concern for art, artists and collectors.

Print clubs are usually run by societies of printmakers producing one or two prints a year and selling on subscription. Prints may be offered as fund-raising devices for good causes, such as promoting training courses or sustaining printmaking studios. Sometimes very eminent artists contribute because they want to support a worthwhile project. These single prints or portfolios are usually good buys; worth keeping, and certainly not worth selling while any copies are still available.

Internet buying

Many individual artists, print workshops, publishers and galleries now offer their wares on the web. This is an increasingly attractive way for the computer-literate to see what is available. It has all the same cautions attached to it as mail order, with the additional problem that the bright light of the computer can make a work look more colourful. It is a wonderful way to browse, internationally. You will see an amazingly wide range of material, though some of it will be fraudulent and some will be plagiarised. I have heard of a picture shown in a gallery window – in this case it was a painting – which had been digitally photographed through the window glass, digitally printed and then offered on the Internet under a different name – and in an edition!

Information which should be available in galleries, on the Internet and at exhibitions

Certain basic information should always be readily available to the print buyer; but it is not always offered, so it is up to the buyer to ask. As we have seen in earlier sections, definitions and terms can be vague and misleading. There are doubtful editions around and even outright fakes, though these are only in the higher price brackets (it is not worth going to the time and expense of producing convincing fakes unless the item is very expensive). Collectors will not be interested in reproduction prints, because these have no inherent value. Sometimes a fan club will gather around an artist such as Sir William Russell-Flint: reproductions of his drawings and watercolours of titillating nudes do have a resale market, though reputable auction houses and galleries will not sell them. To some extent only the buyer with all the facts about a work at their disposal can tell if a print is what it is made out to be, and so make a reasoned judgement about what it is worth. But there is no standard answer to the equation of value versus desirability.

The information which should be available is as follows:

1. *Artist*. Not only should the artist be named, but a short biography should be available on demand. You may wish to chart the artist's career, find out if other works are in a public collection, discover something of their background and aspirations and assess their potential. There may be books and articles on the artist's work which will help your appreciation.

2. *Title*. Most titles of works of art add to the viewer's understanding and for some artists they are an important element in the work. Some titles are just for identification, while others may be a deliberate clue to the artist's intention, offering the key to a complex work. Some may bear just a number in the place of a title, indicating that they are probably part of a series. Artists also put a number or 'untitled' when they don't want any sort of literary significance or reference to be attached to the work.

3. *Signature*. Catalogues will often say what signature has been used – full name, surname or just initials – and where it is placed. If a coloured pencil or some other unusual medium has been used, this is noted.

4. *Edition*. The size of the edition is obviously important: if a very large edition, 200 or more, has been printed, rarity is unlikely to be a factor in its future value. Some collectors and artists feel very strongly that smaller editions are preferable. The number of artist's proofs and *hors commerce* copies should also be known.

5. *Date*. The date is not always written on a print, but it is important to

Set-aside Fields by Margaret Cannon, 2001. Etching and aquatint on copper, and drypoint on acrylic sheet, 370 x 370 mm (14½ x 14¼ in). Printed and published by the artist in an edition of 20. The artist says, 'The second (drypoint) plate was added to give more definition to the drawing and was printed in a slightly different brown to give richness.'

A New Game (Blue) by Kip Gresham, 2002. Screenprint, 610 x 600 mm (24 x 23 ⅝ in). Printed by the artist and published by the Print Studio, Cambridge in an edition of 10. The paper is a mould-made paper called Somerset.

know when during the career of the artist the print was made. Occasionally a double date is seen, for example, 1959–79: this means that it was started in 1959, put to one side and finally finished in 1979.

6. *Publisher*. Many prints are published by artists themselves, so there may be no corroborating evidence in printed catalogues or reviews. Reputable publishing companies will document each edition fully, and their good name is a guarantee of quality and authenticity.

7. *Printer*. It is reasonable to expect to be told when an artist has collaborated with a printer, and it may add to the interest of the work. Some master printers are so highly regarded that anything coming from their workshop is of interest. It is also known that some printers are prepared to do all the work on behalf of the artist; this does detract from the perceived vigour of the print and eventually its value.

8. *Medium*. It is not always easy to guess what print medium has been used when a print has been framed. Thin screen inks can look remarkably like lithographic inks. Not that any one medium is preferable over another; the important question is whether it has been used well or not. However, the more you know about a work, the better you will understand and enjoy it.

9. *Paper*. The paper on which the image is printed can be of great significance. Multiple editions have sometimes been printed on more than one paper. It was once common practice in Europe to print a very popular image in a small edition on a very expensive paper, a larger edition on good-quality standard printmaking paper and a very large, unsigned edition on machine-made paper.

10. *Size*. The size of both the image and the paper can be significant in identifying a print, particularly if an artist tends to use one title many times: for example, Henry Moore has used *Reclining Figure* on many different images.

11. *Condition*. Auction catalogues, mail-order catalogues and Internet displays should say something about the condition of a print, as you cannot see it immediately to judge for yourself. Any marks, tears or other damage should be recorded.

All this information is essential for two basic reasons: so that the collector can get the fullest enjoyment from the work by knowing the artist and how it was made, and also so that they can judge the present and potential value.

Selling prints

The options are to sell at auction, through a gallery, on the Internet or privately.

Any references in catalogues, articles or previous exhibitions should be kept with the receipt or invoice from the seller; if you sell the work later, this information will be valuable in determining authenticity.

Some publishers issue a certificate of authenticity with each sale, though there is no legal requirement to do so and many such certificates are grudging with the sort of information listed above. The more the knowledgeable public ask the important questions, the more even minor galleries as well as artists themselves will become professional in selling works of art.

Whichever way you choose to sell, any information you have been able to collect about the artist and the work will be invaluable. Obviously, it also pays to have kept the work in good condition. If you sell through someone else, such as at auction or through a gallery, you will have to pay commission; but at least the work is more likely to reach its target audience. By selling on the Internet, you are offering the work to the widest-possible audience, but you may also be worried about the security of either the image (it can be downloaded) or the money transaction. There are virtual galleries specialising in selling prints on the Internet which have set up reliable money-transfer systems.

Through my Eyes by Dorothea Wight HonRE, 1997. Mezzotint and aquatint, 197 x 180 mm (7 ¾ x 7 ¼ in). Printed from two plates and published by the artist in an edition of 50.

Sources of Information

Print collections

Many countries have national collections of prints held at a central location, such as the Bibliothèque Nationale in Paris or the Australian National Print Collection in Canberra. British collections are divided between the British Museum, Tate Britain and the Victoria and Albert Museum in London, though major collections are also held at The Hunterian Museum, Glasgow, The Cecil Higgins Museum, Bedford, Cartwright Hall Art Gallery, Bradford, and a number of others. Some other museums have departments of mixed works on paper. It is worth exploring your nearest museum and consulting annual directories on museums, which list their various departments and specialities. If you want to see a particular print or group of works you must apply in advance to the curator, because most collections are kept in storage and the museum staff need notice to get things ready for you. In my experience they are very helpful, but you must have a specific objective in mind. Some institutions will ask for an ID, and, very rarely, an introduction from someone known to the museum is required – from, say, a similar body, such as a university or further education college.

Private collections of a single artist's work may be kept by the artist's family or by a trust set up for that purpose. The Henry Moore Foundation, which under normal circumstances is open by appointment only, is one example of a trust of this kind.

Libraries

Some large libraries have their own print collection, such as the New York City Library or the Library of Congress in Washington. These libraries tend to manage their collections in the same way as museums: though they may also have print exhibitions on the premises open to the public, the collections are for serious study purposes. Public libraries often have a specialist book collection: for example, the Westminster Reference Library in London holds the art-book collection for London. The National Art Library in Britain is held at the Victoria and Albert Museum, and includes books, art magazines, exhibition catalogues, catalogues raisonnés, posters for exhibitions and other information. Public libraries in Britain also have an efficient inter-loan service to get you books from other libraries.

Catalogues raisonnés are a particularly important source for information, as they list and illustrate all the prints made by an artist. They give details of size, edition size and very often the paper, printer and number of colours used for each image. All this helps with accurate identification.

Hacienda or Country Mansion by George Scharf, 1824. This print is typical of the numerous topographical subjects which were published as new territories were colonised. This scene is in Chile.
© The British Museum/ Heritage-Images.

The following list suggests some useful titles for the exploration of printmaking and collecting:

History of printmaking

Adhemar, Jean, *Twentieth Century Graphics*, New York, Praeger, 1971. Comments on some of the most famous prints, mainly from the École de Paris.

Carey, Frances & Griffiths, Antony, *Avant-garde British Printmaking, 1914–1960*, London, British Museum Press, 1990.

Castleman, Riva, *Prints of the Twentieth Century: a History*, London, Thames and Hudson, 1976. Based on the superb collection of prints in the Museum of Modern Art, New York.

Eichenberg, Fritz, *The Art of the Print: Masterpieces, History, Techniques*, London, Thames and Hudson, 1976. An extensive survey of all forms of printmaking with a full bibliography.

Garton, Robin, *British Printmakers, 1855–1955*, Devizes, Garton & Co., 1992. A very useful reference work.

Godfrey, Richard T., *Printmaking in Britain*, Oxford, Phaidon, 1978. A general history from its beginnings to the present day.

Hamilton, James, *Wood engraving & the woodcut in Britain, 1890–1990*, London, Barrie & Jenkins, 1994. An excellent history of xylography.

Man, Felix H. *150 Years of Artists' Lithographs, 1803–1953*, London, Heinemann, 1953. History based on the author's fine collection, now in the Australian National Gallery.

Tallman, Susan, *The Contemporary Print, from Pre-Pop to Postmodern*, London, Thames & Hudson, 1996.

Catalogues raisonnés

Coppel, Stephen, *Linocuts of the Machine Age: Claude Flight and His Followers*, Aldershot, Scolar Press, 1995.

Cramer, Gérald, Grant, Alistair, Mitchinson, David & Cramer, Patrick, *Henry Moore: the Graphic Works 1931–1984* (in four volumes), Geneva, Cramer, 1973–88.

Heenk, Liesbeth & Rosenthal, Nan, *Howard Hodgkin Prints*, London, Thames & Hudson, 2003.

Kinsman, Jane, *The Prints of R.B. Kitaj*, Aldershot, Scolar Press, 1994.

Levinson, Orde, *Quality and Experiment: the Prints of John Piper*, London, Lund Humphries, 1996.

Wiseman, Caroline, *Elisabeth Frink: Original Prints*, London, Art Books International, 1998.

Print workshops

Brown, Kathan, *Ink, Paper, Metal, Wood*, San Francisco, Chronicle Books, 1996, A vivid account of working with artists at Crown Point Press.

Gilmour, Pat, *Artists at Curwen*, London, Tate Gallery, 1977.

Sidey, Tessa, *Editions Alecto: Original Graphics, Multiple Originals, 1960–1981*, Aldershot, Lund Humphries, 2003.

Collecting

Buchsbaum, Ann, *A Practical Guide to Print Collecting*, New York, Van
  Nostrand Reinhold, 1975. Mainly concerned with collecting pre-20th
  century prints, but also includes a useful list of catalogues raisonnés.
Gascoigne, Bamber, *How to Identify Prints*, London Thames & Hudson,
  1987, revised in 2004. An excellent guide to recognising different kinds
  of old prints, though not the most recent developments.
Griffiths, Antony (ed.), *Landmarks in Print Collecting: Connoisseurs and
  Donors at the British Museum since 1753*, London, British Museum, 1996
Ivins, William M., Cohn, Marjorie B., *How Prints Look*, Boston, Beacon
  Press, 1987. A guide to the collector.
Rosen, Randy, *Prints, the Facts and Fun of Collecting*, New York, E. P. Dutton,
  1978. An excellent and well-informed introduction to print collecting.

Printmaking techniques

The best books on the printmaking techniques used today are published
by A&C Black. The *Printmaking Handbooks* series is ongoing, inexpensive,
well illustrated, and written by practising artists who are leaders in their
chosen fields. The titles published to date are: *Collagraphs, Inks, Creating
Artists' Books, Printmaking for Beginners, Etching and Photopolymer Intaglio
Techniques, Traditional Techniques in Contemporary Chinese Printmaking, Relief
Printmaking, Japanese Woodblock Printing, Stone Lithography, Plate Lithography,
Digital Printmaking*, and *Dictionary of Printmaking Terms*, and in preparation
are: *Japanese Popular Street Prints, Monoprinting, Colour Printmaking,
Papermaking for Printmakers, Photo-based Printmaking Preparation,
Printmaking with Found Objects* and *Intaglio*. Another title from the same
publishers but in a slightly larger-format series is *Handmade Prints* by Anne
Desmet and Jim Anderson. This is a great if you want to try printmaking
at home with easily available materials and without the need for a press.

Magazines and newspapers

Prints rarely feature in newspapers, excepting the occasional obituary of an
artist who was known as a printmaker. Art magazines covering all art media
are not a regular source of critical articles on artist's original prints, but they
do advertise galleries and museums showing print exhibitions. The best-
known quarterly magazine is *Printmaking Today*, ISSN 0960 9253,
www.printmakingtoday.co.uk, which, though mainly read by artists, gives
international coverage of exhibitions, public collections, galleries and books.

Practical study

One of the best ways of gaining a deeper understanding of printmaking is to
attend classes at a local further-education college. Explanations in books can
give some idea of a technique, but cannot convey the physical sensation of
cutting wood, drawing on copper or mixing ink. Many print societies run by a
group of printmakers also give classes introducing the public to techniques
and print appreciation; occasionally, museums give a similar hands-on
experience, though usually only for children. Some professional print
workshops run special classes, often for a day only, on a particular technique.
These classes enable artists to refresh their techniques and to try new ones.

Glossary

Acid. A corrosive liquid used to etch metal plates: nitric and hydrochloric acids, along with ferric chloride, a salt, are the most commonly used mordants in intaglio printmaking. Various acids are also used in lithography to desensitise areas, and an alkali, caustic soda, is used to etch lino.

Acid-free. pH is expressed on a scale 0–14, from acidity to alkalinity; pH7 is neutral. Used with particular reference to paper, boards and paste, which should all be acid-free for fine printmaking and framing.

Affiche originale. Used in France to denote a poster created by an artist for their own exhibition or for a group exhibition. They are frequently signed, and sometimes numbered if only a few were made, and are usually lithographs or screenprints. There are collectors who specialise in these valuable posters.

All-digital prints. Images made by a computer-controlled output device without using any traditional non-digital methods.

Aluminium. This metal was introduced for lithographic plates in 1891, though today it is usually part of an alloy. It can be etched and used for intaglio plates, but it does have the drawback of oxidising very easily.

Antiquarian. A paper size approximately 790 x 1350 mm (31 x 53 in). It was first made in 1774 by papermaker James Whatman II (1741–98).

Aquatint. An intaglio technique which uses a fine resin dust adhering to the plate in the areas where tones are required. The resin is an acid-resist, so only areas around the dust particles are bitten. Plates can be etched to varying depths, thus holding more or less ink, resulting in a wide range of tones expressed in a random pattern. The resin dust is often replaced today by the safer use of sprayed, black, oil-based ink droplets, which when dry also resist acid.

Archival inks. Coloured printing inks expected to last without fading for 10–50 years, black ink for 100 years. Artists producing original prints have demanded archival inks for ink-jet printers; these inks have greatly improved in recent years, but are not yet widely used by commercial *giclée* printers.

Archival paper and board. Acid-free materials must be used to ensure long-term stability and purity. The mounting boards are also called museum boards.

Artist's book. A book, or a work in the form of a book, or a sequence of images gathered together, designed in its entirety by the artist and produced in a small edition using printmaking techniques. Often a

Approaching St Kilda by Joseph Winkelman PPRE. Aquatint, 380 x 540 mm (15 x 21¼in.). Printed from a copperplate and published by the artist in an edition of 150.

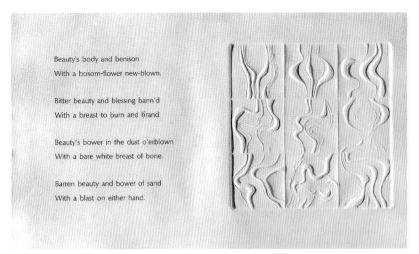

Beauty's body and benison
With a bosom-flower new-blown.

Bitter beauty and blessing bann'd
With a breast to burn and brand.

Beauty's bower in the dust o'erblown
With a bare white breast of bone.

Barren beauty and bower of sand
With a blast on either hand.

Beauty's Body and Benison by Birgit Skiold, 1969. Blind-embossed intaglio print from lino, 230 x 230 mm (9 x 9 in). This double-page spread comes from the artist's book *Chimes*, poems by Dante Gabriel Rossetti (1828–1882): its letterpress text was hand-printed by Derek Redfern; the embossed linocuts were printed by the artist; and the book was published by Circle Press Publications in an edition of 75.

collection of prints with supporting text, issued on subscription. The production may be a collaboration with a bookbinder and other technicians. It was once a predominantly European tradition, but is now widespread.

Artist's proof. Copies of a print identical to the edition, but reserved for the exclusive use of the artist for archives, sale or gifts. Normally, these are not more than 10 per cent of the edition size. Signed by the artist on the left-hand side beneath the image: 'artist's proof' ('AP') or in France *épreuve d'artiste* ('EA').

Artist's original print. See p13.

Auto-. As a prefix to a print medium, indicates that the artist created the printing matrix; originally used to differentiate an artist's work from commercial reproduction without the use of photography, as in, for example, autolithography.

Authorised edition. See Estate print.

Avant les lettres. As seen on old prints, meaning the state of the print before the title and the names of artist, engraver and publisher were added beneath the image; in other words, the state before editioning.

Baxter print or Baxtertype. In 1835, George Baxter (1804–1867) patented a system with a monochrome aquatint key-plate to which he added up to 20 woodblocks printed in colour. These are examples of mixed-media prints.

Bite. The corrosive action of acid on metal.

Bled image. When the image is printed right to the edge of the paper or the margins are cut off. Also called a 'bleed print'.

Bleeding colour. Ink which spreads beyond the printed area leaving a halo effect. Usually this means the ink is too thin, thus enabling it to seep into the surrounding soft paper fibres. It is not considered good printing technique, but on occasion artists may artificially produce it by spraying the back of the paper with solvent before the ink is dry. It is also a technique seen in Asian water-based printing (see *Bokashi*).

Blended colours. When two or more colours are blended together. This can be done by rolling separate colours on an ink slab until they blend together or by doing the same thing with a squeegee in screen-printing. Also called 'rainbow' or 'merged' colours and, in machine lithography, a 'split duct'.

Blind embossing. When an uninked block or plate is forced into dampened paper, leaving a 3D image. This is normally done on an etching press, which has a high pressure, or it can be done by hand, working from the back of the paper and using a rounded point to mould the paper into the incised design of the block.

Blind stamp. See Chop mark.

Board. Any paper that is heavier than 90lb per ream (500 sheets) or 220 gsm (grams per square metre).

Bokashi. A Japanese woodblock technique that allows colour on the block to be thinned with water at an edge so that, using capillary action, it fades in the direction of the wood grain.

Bon à tirer. French for 'good to print' (the same as 'passed for press'), it instructs a printer to print the edition using this agreed proof as a guide. Also written as 'BAT'. These proofs are of special interest and sometimes appear on the market.

Bookplate. A label denoting ownership of a book, pasted inside the cover. Bookplates that are wood engravings, woodcuts or linocuts, and not commercially printed, are considered to be a special corner of print collecting.

Boxwood. A hard, close-grained wood used for wood engraving on the end grain. It was also used for large-size letterpress display type. This wood is increasingly difficult to find, and expensive, so fruit-woods are sometimes used, or even a resin substitute.

BSI. British Standards Institute. Its *Classification of Prints* was published in 1996. See p18.

Bubblejet printer. A type of drop-on-demand ink-jet printer.

Buffered paper. An alkaline additive of calcium or magnesium carbonate to paper pulp ensures that the finished sheet of paper is of neutral pH.

Burin. A group of steel engraving tools, also called 'gravers', with pointed, elliptical or lozenge-shaped tips used on metal and wood. The word is interchangeable with 'engraving' and also describes the typical line that results from engraving.

Burnishing.
1. Applying pressure by rubbing on the back of paper laid on an inked relief block. The Japanese use a circular pad called a *baren*; the Chinese printing pad is a long rectangle called a *ca zi*; and in the West artists use the back of a wooden spoon, a rounded pebble or something similar which can be hand-held.
2. Rubbing down the aquatint or mezzotint texture on an intaglio plate to lighten a tonal area by using a smooth, slightly curved metal tool and oil to lubricate.

Burr.
1. The intaglio term for the roughened edge of metal on each side of a scratched or drypoint line. The burr holds ink as well as the intaglio mark; the velvety quality is a characteristic of drypoint and mezzotint. The burr wears rapidly during printing, so if many copies are required the plate must be steel-faced.
2. The texture produced by a mezzotint rocker.

Cael., caelvit. Latin for 'engraved this', as seen on old prints where the person who engraved the plate was usually different from the artist who originated the image.

Calcographia. Deriving from the Spanish/Italian word for copper engraving (*calcografia*), this is a portmanteau word that includes all forms of printmaking and is

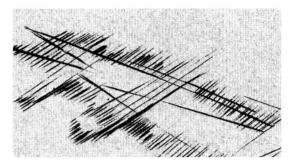

Enlarged detail from *Jumbo Jet* by Anne Breivik (see p47) showing the characteristic engraved line and the burr holding the ink. Many engravers remove the burr, giving a very clean mark, but in this case it enhances the atmosphere of the image.

used by museums and for collections of prints.

Cancellation. When the edition has been completed, the printing matrix is cancelled to ensure that another cannot be printed. It is defaced in some way by drilling a hole, scoring a cross or using acid. A cancellation proof is then pulled as evidence. The practice has lapsed in recent years.

Carbon print. An early form of photogravure invented in the mid-19th century and recently revived by artists wanting to use photography and intaglio techniques.

Carborundum print. Silicon carbide grit is glued to a backing sheet to make a very deeply textured intaglio plate characteristically holding a heavy ink load. Carborundum printing is a collagraph technique.

Card. A lightweight machine-made board not used as a printing substrate but to make relief matrices for card prints; also called 'card cuts' and 'cardboard cuts'.

Cardboard. A general term for boards 15 mm ($\frac{1}{16}$ in) or thicker.

Cartridge paper. A tough machine-made paper, uncoated but surface-sized, weighing anywhere in the range 90–220 gsm. Used by printmakers for preliminary designs and proofing but not for the edition.

Cast-paper print. The term is used for a blind embossed print but more commonly for a print for which the paper has been specially made or cast, often in an irregular shape, incorporating coloured pulp and deep textures. Areas of the paper may then be printed, or collaged printed elements added. Usually entirely made by the papermaker/printmaker. The print is classified as a mixed-media work. See p61.

Catalogue raisonné. A comprehensive scholarly catalogue of an artist's complete works, giving title, date, medium, edition size, physical size, paper, printer and publisher.

Chiaroscuro woodcut. An early form of colour printing from wood using three or more separate blocks. The darkest colour was used to print the main or key block, and lighter tones of the same colour were added to give the impression of 3D.

China paper. A thin, strong paper (called *chine* in French), also called 'India paper' because it was imported by the East India Company. Today it is machine-made and used for Bibles and reference books.

Chine collé. A French term for a thin paper, usually of Asian origin, which is glued or collaged onto a heavier paper. It is often seen just in the image area of a print, giving it a subtle background different from the margins. Sometimes artists use smaller, irregular pieces of paper beneath the printing to add extra colours; these pieces may also be pre-printed. It is usually an intaglio technique.

Chop mark. A blind embossed stamp in the corner of a print denoting the artist, printer or publisher.

Chromiste. French for a craftsman who interprets a design by another hand to create a relief, intaglio, lithograph or screenprint.

Chromolithography. Colour lithography drawn by a *chromiste*; 'chromo' for short in English. When the term was first coined in the early 19th century, it meant specifically colour-crayon lithography.

Cliché verre. French for a glass print. A drawing is made on a darkened sheet of glass using an etching needle. This negative drawing is used like a film negative to make a photographic print.

Clipped. A print that has been trimmed close to the image area leaving no margins. The plate mark on early intaglio prints was often trimmed off.

CMYK. The four standard process colours (cyan, magenta, yellow and black) used in commercial printing to reproduce a tonal image such as a colour photograph.

Collage. From the French word *coller*, meaning 'to stick or glue'; used in printmaking it means to prepare a printing block or to assemble a print from various elements.

Collagraph. A print, intaglio and/or relief, taken from a

Smoke/Flower by Paul Coldwell, 2004. Collotype and screenprint, 270 x 330 mm (10⅞ x 13 in). Printed and published by Paul Thirkell at the University of the West of England Centre for Fine Print Research in an edition of seven. The artist says, '*The images were made on a computer bringing together a photographic image of the bombing of Iraq and a drawing of flowers made on the computer, both using the Photoshop program. The image was made in layers, enabling the printer to print the dot layer as a screen print on top of the collotype plate printed intaglio. The image is part of a series of three.*'

collaged matrix. A backing plate of metal, board, card, plastic or wood forms the base. Materials such as cut-out shapes, found objects and organic substances can be glued to the base. Drawn elements can be modelled in glue, paste or gesso, to which carborundum grit, sand, etc., can be added to give tooth to printing ink. Absorbent materials are sealed before printing.

Collogravure. French for a 'collagraph'.

Collograph. Often a misspelling of 'collagraph'. Used mostly in the US. Confusingly, it is also used to describe a collotype made by an artist, as opposed to a commercial collotype.

Collotype. A photomechanical process invented in the mid-19th century to make fine reproductions. A coating of a light-sensitive gelatin (colloid) on a glass sheet is exposed to a photographic negative and then developed. Hardened areas of gelatin accept ink when rolled up, but the less-exposed soft parts reject ink. Natural reticulations in the gelatin give an aquatint-like texture, and no screen is required to reproduce a full and delicate tonal range. Recently some printmakers have revived this almost extinct process to make collographs.

Colour fading. A gradual change in the colour of paper due to its acid content and of ink due to exposure to light. Printmakers aim to use inks and pigments that have the best colour fastness. The colour industry uses the Blue Wool Scale (BWS) to measure lightfastness, graded from eight, which is permanent, to one, which is very fugitive. Another colour scale has been developed called Delta E, but like BWS it depends on exposing printed material in controlled lab conditions; it is hard to relate these systems to real-life conditions. Generally, reds fade first, then yellows, while blue and black last for much longer. See the British Standards Institute publication *Classification of Prints* (p18).

Colour proof. A pull taken to check the colours and their registration prior to editioning, and also to check the order of printing of the different colours.

Colour saturation. The strength or intensity of a colour.

Colour scanner. An electronic device which digitally records a colour image.

Colour separation. Where an image is broken down into a number of colours for printing, usually as one colour per printing matrix. Separations can also be drawn on tracing paper as a guide to making each matrix or when using the reduction method.

Coloured print. Usually printed in a monochrome ink, colour is added by hand, traditionally in watercolour, to each print.

Computer print. See Digital print.

Continuous tone. The smooth graduation from light to dark tones rendered by variable density, as in a photograph; in collotype, where the tone is created by random reticulation; in stochastic printing by a random dot screen, in intaglio by aquatint and mezzotint; and it also refers to the random-grain texture of lithographic stone or grained plate.

Copperplate. A general term for all intaglio plates and prints. A copperplate press is the same as an etching or intaglio press.

Copyright. The print copyright belongs to the publisher, who may also be the artist, unless otherwise agreed. The idea, rather than the finished print, belongs to the artist and is known as the artist's intellectual property.

Counterproof. A wet proof that is pressed onto another sheet of paper, it will be in reverse. They are sometimes seen at auctions, regarded as curiosities.

Crayon-manner engraving. An 18th-century technique intended to mimic the texture of a crayon drawing through the use of needles and roulettes on an intaglio plate.

Crevé. A French term for an etching in which the space between closely drawn lines is overetched and lost.

Cross-hatching. Crossing lines drawn to depict a tonal area. Difficult to maintain in etching as the metal between the lines tends to break down.

Cross media. Describes works combining more than one discipline, such as print and video, print and architecture or print and music.

Crown. A traditional paper size, 380 x 508 mm (15 x 20 in).

Cushion. A small sand-filled leather bag on which a metal plate or woodblock rests during engraving. The plate or block can be easily turned for the purposes of engraving curved lines.

Cut. A print taken from any cut or engraved surface, such as a woodcut or linocut.

Cylinder press. A press where the top roller provides the pressure, such as an intaglio press, a letterpress or a proof press.

Cylinder press with a zinc intaglio plate on the press bed. A sheet of paper will be placed on the inked plate; the felts, here seen resting on the pressure roller, will be folded over the paper; and the press bed will be run through when the handle is turned.

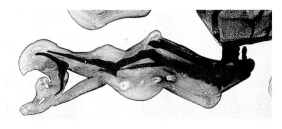

Diazo lithography. An enlarged area showing the continuous-tone textures.

Deckle. The thin, irregular edge of a sheet of handmade paper. An imitation of this effect can be created on cheaper papers.

Deep etch. The very deep biting of an intaglio plate in acid, sometimes right through the metal.

Delineavit. Latin for 'drew this', as seen on old prints. Often abbreviated to *del.*, *delt.* or *delin.*

Depôt legal. French term for the compulsory deposit of prints at the Bibliothèque Nationale in Paris.

Dessiné. French for 'drawn', as seen on old prints.

Diazo lithography. Also called 'continuous-tone lithography'. An image drawn on grained transparent film and exposed to a positive-working diazo plate is broken into minute particles by the grain on the plate, and on the film, giving a continuous tone without the use of a dot screen. 'Diazo' is the term given to a group of light-sensitive compounds.

Die stamping. Embossing paper between two metal plates, one in relief and one in intaglio.

Digital halftone. Two kinds of computer-originated halftone can be made: AM (amplitude-modulated), where the dots are on a grid similar to photographically screened halftones, and FM (frequency-modulated), which uses a random pattern of dots similar to continuous tone.

Digital print. A print which has been created wholly or in part using digital equipment.

Dimensional stability. Paper or film which is not distorted by environmental changes such as humidity. This can be important when printing different colours over several days.

Direct lithographic press. A press where the paper is in direct contact with the inked stone or plate. The earliest kind of lithographic press, it is still being used by artists today. Commercial lithographic printing has used the faster offset press since 1904.

Direct lithographic press. Stanley Jones proofing in the Curwen Studio. In the middle distance Garrick Palmer is drawing on a zinc lithographic plate.

Dolly. A small pad of cloth or roll of felt used to dab coloured inks into small areas of a block (relief) or plate (intaglio) in multicoloured printing.

Dotted print. *Manière criblée* (French), *Schrotblatt* (German). A 15th-century technique in which a metal plate is engraved and indented with goldsmith's tools and then printed in relief.

Double elephant. A size of paper favoured by printmakers, 1020 x 690 mm (40 x 27 in).

Dry brush. A technique whereby distinct brush marks are made using almost dry lithographic ink (tusche), varnish or screen filler.

Dry pigments. Powdered pigments that are mixed with various vehicles to make printing inks for different forms of printmaking.

Drypoint. *Point seché* (French), *Kaltnadel* (German). An intaglio engraving technique whereby the image is drawn on a metal or plastic plate using a hard point called a 'drypoint needle'. Sealed card or card with a plastic finish can also be used for drypoint and is strong enough to yield a few prints; it is useful for experiments and beginners. The action of the point throws up a burr on either side of the line which holds the ink, giving the characteristic velvety line; this soon wears down, so metal plates are usually steel-faced if an edition of more than a dozen prints is required. See p48.

DTP. Desktop publishing, a general term for the use of a computer to lay out type and images, a widely used technology for making artist's books.

Dye. A solution of fine pigment particles dissolved in a binder and always in suspension. Used in ink-jet printers and to make DIY screen inks cheaply. The colours are not usually very lightfast.

Eau forte. French for 'nitric acid', for which in English the archaic term is 'aqua fortis', it literally translates as 'strong water'; it is also a collective term for all forms of etching.

Edition. The declared number of prints published, not including artist's proofs and other proofs. There should be no further printing of that image.

Edition de luxe. An edition or part of an edition printed on special paper, often with a watermark signature of the artist and presented in a luxurious portfolio.

Editioning. The printing of the edition once a proof has been passed for press by the artist.

Summer Rain by Anita Klein PRE, 2003. Drypoint on aluminium, 410 x 305mm (16 ⅛ x 12 in). Printed and published by the artist in an edition of 25.

Editor's proof. A final print, identical to the edition, is reserved for the editor who has organised the publication of an image or suite of images, particularly when a number of artists are contributing to a suite.

Electrotype. A metal duplicate printing plate, often made from delicate wood engravings, linocuts or fragile metal type which would not stand up to the pressure of a printing press.

Electrolytic etching. An etching process whereby an electric charge is passed from an anode attached to a printing plate of the same metal as the anode and suspended in a weak acid bath (copper sulphate for copperplates). Metal is etched from the plate where it is not protected by an acid resist such as varnish, wax, thick printing ink or aquatint.

Electrostatic printing. Photocopying and laser-printing process whereby the image is formed in electrical charges which attract toner particles; these are then transferred to a substrate such as paper and fixed by heat. Not archival in quality and so not suitable for artist's original prints.

Untitled by Thomas Bewick, c. 1780. Wood engraving, 38 x 72 mm (1 ½ x 2 - in). This end-grain wood engraving was a printer's stock block for use as a chapter heading or end piece in books.

Embossing. *Gaufrage* (French), *Blindrucke* (German), *Karazuri* or *Kimekoni* (Japanese). A deep, 3D impression on paper; printed with or without ink from a deeply cut or etched plate on a heavyweight dampened paper.

Emulsion. A light-sensitive coating on photographic paper, film or a printing matrix such as a screen.

End grain. A block of hardwood, traditionally box-wood, cut across the trunk and showing the growth rings; used for finely worked wood engravings.

Engraving. An image cut into a metal plate (without the use of acid), wood, lino or other material by means of tools such as a graver, burin, knife, gouge, drypoint needle or electrical craft tool. It is also a general word for an incised mark or an incised block, and even a general term for any artist's print.

Épreuve d'artiste. French for an 'artist's proof', shortened to EA.

Estampe. French general term for an intaglio print. Also used to designate a print in which a copyist has made the printing matrices after an original by another hand, similar to a *chromiste* in lithography. Sometimes used to describe a print that relies on embossing.

Estampille. French term for a 'run-on print', extra to the edition, unsigned, and used for advertising purposes or records.

Estate print. A print issued after the artist's death either by the family or trustees. Usually distinguished by a special blind stamp or chop mark.

Etching. *Eau forte* (French), *Radierung* (German). A print taken from a metal plate etched in acid. The term is also used loosely to mean all intaglio prints.

Etching ground. The acid-resistant coat of wax, black printing ink or acrylic copolymer on a metal plate, through which the design is drawn (line etching) or impressed (soft ground).

Ex. coll. Latin for 'from the collection of'. Used to establish the provenance of a work.

Excudit. Latin for 'engraved this' (followed by the name of the publisher), as seen on old prints beneath the title and other details.

Exposure unit. In photo-based printmaking, a light-sensitive surface is put in contact with a negative (or positive) on a vacuum bed and exposed to a light source for a measured time. It is used to make photo-stencils, photolitho plates, photopolymer, photo-intaglio and photo-relief plates.

Facsimile. A fine-quality reproduction exactly the same size as the original.

False biting. See Foul biting.

Fecit. Latin for 'made this', as found on old prints, which give the name of the engraver, etcher or litho-grapher who interpreted the artist's original design.

Fillers. Thick liquids or solids which are used to fill the spaces between the threads of screen meshes. The liquids are usually PVA-based, but they may also be cellulose-, oil- or water-based, or glue. Solids include crayon or powder in the form of talc or fuller's earth.

Fillet. A strip of wood or other material used in a picture frame to produce a space between the print and the glass so that the two do not touch when a window mount is not used.

Film. The transparent plastic strip or sheet used as a carrier for photographic emulsion. Clear acetate sheet is used by printmakers to check registration and to cut stencils or masks. Grained plastic sheet is used to draw on to make positives and negatives for photo-based techniques.

Flattening. Paper which has been dampened for printing must then be flattened to prevent cockling. This is usually done by interleaving each print with acid-free tissue and absorbent blotting paper and putting the resulting sandwich under pressure; the blotters are changed until the prints are dry. Prints that have cockled can be dampened and treated in the same way.

Flax. Plant fibre, in the form of linen rags, was the principal constituent of paper – hence, rag paper. The collection of rags was once a considerable industry;

they were sorted, cleaned, cut up and beaten to make paper pulp. New flax fibre is now being used to make paper.

Flexography. Line block or halftone made from rubber, plastic compounds or photopolymers; cheaper than metal. It is widely used in the printing of commercial packaging, but there is also a much-refined use by artists called 'photopolymer intaglio' or 'photopolymer relief', or sometimes 'flexo' for short. See also Solar prints.

Flock. Powdered wool or other fibres glued to a relief-block surface to hold diluted inks or dyes when printing on textiles.

Flock print. A 15th-century technique whereby an image is printed with glue and flock is dusted over it giving it a velvety texture. It is occasionally used by artists today, though the technique has been updated so that synthetic fibres are fired from a gun onto the sticky surface of the print.

Flour. Wheat flour is sometimes used instead of rice flour to make a paste for attaching *chine collé* and paper hinges.

Fluorescent inks. A group of inks that absorb light and re-emit it.

Foil. Metallic foils can be used on prints in a similar way to *chine collé*. See p63.

Formschneider. German for an artisan who cuts a woodcut or engraving following another artist's design. Similar to a *chromiste*.

Foul biting. When an intaglio ground lifts off because the acid is too strong or the ground was not well applied. The grainy texture left on the exposed metal plate is a quality some artists use to deliberate effect.

Four-colour process. The usual method of colour reproduction whereby a full range of colours is suggested by the optical illusion of printing cyan (turquoise blue), magenta, yellow and black dots. The dot system is called halftone and is measured as so many dots per square inch (dpi). The four colours are shortened to CMYK. Four-colour halftones are used by artists in screen-printing, lithography and intaglio, and also for digital prints, where a colour photograph is required.

Foxing. Discoloured spots on paper due to a type of mildew.

Fractint. A distinctive pattern on an intaglio plate obtained by sandwiching two inked plates together, or an inked plate and a flat surface, and then pulling them apart; the resulting plate is then etched.

Frame. A rectangular structure for protecting a print, consisting of glass, mount, back and moulding. Also, an open rectangle of wood or metal over which a screen mesh is stretched to support a stencil in screen-printing. The frame of a printing press is its structural strength: it supports the bed, rollers, platen, and the scraper bar or screen.

Frottage. French term for rubbing on the back of paper to transfer an inked image to the paper. See also Burnishing.

Fugitive colour. Inks which are not lightfast. See Blue Wool Scale.

Furnish. Papermaker's term for paper pulp.

Gaufrage. French for 'embossing'.

Giclée. French for 'sprayed', initially used to describe fine-art ink-jet prints. The term was adopted by some American artists who wanted to distinguish between commercial ink-jet prints and those that were artist-made. Today, it is almost a derogatory word in printmaking circles, since it is widely used for ink-jet-printed reproductions.

Glass print. An old technique in which a relief or intaglio print on thin paper is stuck onto the back of a sheet of glass, face down. The paper can be peeled off to leave the printed design, which can be hand-coloured.

Gouge. A steel tool used to cut relief blocks; can be either V- or U-shaped.

Gravé. French for 'engraved by', as seen on old prints.

Graver. A steel tool used to engrave lines on wood, metal or plastic. It will cut long lines at a standard depth or by varying the depth the line swells or diminishes. See also Burin.

Gravure. French for engraving. It is also a general word for all forms of printmaking, including, in the past, reproductions.

Ground. See Hard ground, Soft ground and Lift ground.

Group print. Cooperative, mural-sized prints on which several artists collaborate.

Gum arabic. A secretion of several varieties of acacia tree. It is used in solution in lithography to desensitise and etch stone and plates, and acts as a binder in some

Halftone dot screen.

water-based paints. It is also used to make lithographic transfer paper.

Halftone. The optical illusion of continuous tones is rendered by small, variable-sized dots obtained by inserting a cross-ruled screen in front of a negative in a camera. The technique is widely used in commercial printing to reproduce photographs, and by artists when photographic imagery is required. Today the term is also used for stochastic and other random dot screens.

Hand-colouring. Colour added to a print by hand.

Handmade paper. Paper made by hand in single sheets and characterised by a deckle edge all round. It has no distinct grain, as the vatman distributes the paper fibres evenly by shaking the mould.

Hanga. Japanese term for a woodblock print and its printing, now used for any contemporary print.

Hardboard. Compressed wood-fibre board, known as Masonite® in the USA. It is used as a relief-block material (hence 'hardboard cut'), as packing in a relief press and as a general-purpose studio material.

Hard ground. A mixture of wax, bitumen and resin that is used as an acid resist for coating an etching plate. Alternatives are acrylic-based or else black printing ink.

Heat-cutting. Oxyacetylene or other gas torches can be used to cut a design into a metal plate for relief or intaglio printing.

Heliochrome. An early term for a 'three-colour-relief halftone'.

Heliogravure. French for 'photogravure' or 'rotary intaglio printing', once widely used for magazine printing but now mostly superseded by offset lithography.

Heliorelief. A process to make photo-relief blocks on wood or fibreboard.

Heliotype. Another name for 'collotype'.

Hinges. Folded strips of paper used to hold a print in position in a mount or frame. They should be made of a strong but light acid-free paper and used with an acid-free paste.

Holzschnitt. German word for a 'woodcut'.

Hors commerce. French for a print identical to but extra to the edition, used for display or archives. Shortened to HC, literally 'outside commerce'.

Hybrid print. A print combining traditional techniques with photography or digital imaging.

Image. The design or visual elements of a print.

Impasto. Originally an Italian term associated with thickly applied paint, it can be used to mean a 3D intaglio made from a deeply bitten plate or collagraph.

Impermanent resist. An intaglio acid resist used because it will break down in the acid bath, giving an organic and lively mark: diluted bitumen varnish, wax crayons and some felt-tipped pens can be used in this way.

Imperial. Paper size approx. 560 x 760 mm (23 x 30 in); the size can vary from mill to mill.

Imprint. The name and address of a commercial printer required by act of parliament to be printed on all printed matter. Brought in originally as an anti-sedition measure, it is not enforced on small items today.

Impression. A print or proof, and also the pressure required to transfer ink from matrix to paper.

Impression mark. The deeper plate-mark which characterises an intaglio print. Sometimes a light impression can be seen on the back of relief and lithographic prints pulled from stone.

Impressit. Latin for 'printed this', as seen on some old prints.

Incidebat. Latin for 'incised this', as seen on some old prints.

Incunabula. Refers to those early European books produced from the invention of movable type, about 1454, to 1500.

India paper. See China paper.

Indirect stencils. A group of light-sensitive stencils

made first and then applied to a wet screen. They have a polyester backing, which is peeled off after exposure and development, before they are applied to the screen.

Ink. Pigments mixed with a vehicle (such as oil or acrylic), making them suitable for different methods of printing.

Inking. The application of ink to the printing matrix by roller, dabber, scraper, brush or squeegee.

Ink-jet printer. A computer printer which sprays tiny ink droplets onto a substrate such as paper. Bubblejet printers use heat expansion to create the pressure to drive the ink droplets; other printers use piezo electrical charges. The best-quality printers give near continuous-tone quality.

Ink-jet, solid. An ink-jet printer which uses solid wax sticks of ink, which are melted and then sprayed onto a transfer drum. Gives brilliant but not very permanent colours.

Ink knife. A steel knife or spatula or wedge shape used to mix ink to the desired colour or consistency.

Ink slab. A non-porous slab of glass, stone, plastic or metal used to roll out ink prior to inking the matrix.

Input devices. Computer keyboard, mouse and scanner.

Insurance copy. Some print publishers have an extra copy or two printed in case an edition copy is damaged; a recent practice adopted by some mail-order publishers.

Intaglio. Originally from the Italian word *intagliare*, meaning to incise or engrave a design into a surface.

Intaglio press. A sturdy metal cylinder press which can exert pressure of about five tons per sq. in, thus sucking out the printing ink in the incisions of an intaglio plate and depositing it onto a substrate. Also called a 'copperplate', 'cylinder' or 'etching' press.

Intaglio print. A print from an incised surface where the ink lies in the etched or engraved parts and not on the plate surface. The following are all intaglio prints: etchings, engravings, aquatints, mezzotints, drypoints; some of these techniques may be used in combination on the same plate.

Internal sizing. Size is added to paper pulp before sheet formation.

Invenit. Latin for 'designed this', as seen on some old prints.

My Balcony in Verona by Carmen Gracia RE, 1997. Intaglio, 370 x 331 mm (14¾ x 13 in). Printed and published by the artist in an edition of 75.

Iris printer. The trade name for a continuous ink-jet printer that by overlaying CMYK can produce 16 million different colours because each dot can be varied in size. Some versions have extra colours added. Some artists who use this form of printing make the creative choice of calling their prints 'Iris prints' in preference to *giclée*, which is associated with reproductions.

ISO. International Organisation for Standardisation measurement for the metric weight of paper is shown in grams per square metre (gsm or gm2). ISO sizes for printing paper start at A0, which is 841 x 1189 mm, while A1 is 594 x 841 mm, A2 is 420 x 594 mm, and so on.

Jigsaw. A system for printing several colours together. Blocks or plates are cut up, the pieces inked separately and then reassembled for printing.

Kento. A traditional Japanese system for registering printing paper onto a series of blocks in colour printing; widely adopted by Western relief printmakers.

Key image. In colour printing it is the matrix which has the most work, the outline, or that part of the colour separation which pulls the whole image together. It is printed first during proofing so that the other colours may be registered to it, but is frequently printed last during editioning thus coming on top of the other colours. Sometimes the key image is used during proofing to check registration but then discarded.

Laid down. A lithograph drawn on transfer paper is 'laid down' onto a stone or plate for printing.

Laid paper. The earliest European paper shows laid lines running the length of the sheet. Chain lines run across; these are made by the binding wire or thread holding the laid wires in place on the mould. The impression of these wires can be seen when the sheet is held up to the light. The effect is created in machine-made paper by a dandy roll taken over the wet pulp. See also Wove paper.

Laser printer. A computer printer in which a laser beam transfers an electrical charge onto a drum, which passes through a powdered pigment before being transferred to a substrate and fused by heat. Four passes transfer CMYK in turn; some models deposit the toner on an intermediary surface first.

Laser-transfer paper. Similar to ceramic-transfer paper but made to withstand the heat in a laser printer. The paper is used by artists to transfer images onto canvas, to transfer preprinted images, or as a resist on a photo-intaglio plate.

Lavis. French term for a 'lithographic wash', which has characteristic reticulations.

Leaf. A sheet of paper which is printed on both sides.

Letterpress. Surface printing from metal type and process-engraved blocks. Now no longer commercial except on a very small scale, but still treasured by the private-press movement and makers of artist's books.

Lift ground. See Sugar lift.

Light-sensitive coating. Chemicals which react to light by hardening in exposed areas. These chemicals are coated onto paper, glass, metal and screen meshes; they produce an acid-resist for etching relief and intaglio blocks, a grease-attracting surface in lithography and a mesh sealer in screen-printing.

Light source. The sun, the photoflood, as well as mercury-vapour, quartz-halide, metal-halide and sun lamps are all used by artists as light sources in photo-based printmaking.

Limited edition. A printing run of a predetermined length that is not exceeded or reprinted. Each print is signed and numbered by the artist to guarantee its

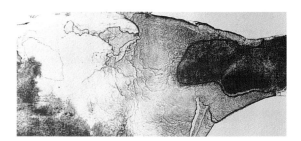

Enlarged detail of a lithographic wash.

quality and that the edition is limited to the declared number.

Line block. A photo-etched relief block for letterpress printing, consisting of lines and solid areas, and no halftones. Also called 'line cut', 'line engraving', 'line etching' or 'line plate'.

Linocut. *Gravure sur linoleum* (French), *Linoschnitt* (German). Engraving on linoleum.

lith. Greek for 'stone' or 'the lithographer', as seen on old prints.

Lithography. Derived from the Greek *lithos*, meaning 'stone', and graphos, meaning drawing. Invented in Munich in 1796 by Aloys Senefelder, the technique is based on the antipathy of grease and water.

Machine-made paper. See p76.

Maculature. A second impression taken from a printing matrix without re-inking; usually done to remove excess ink. They do sometimes appear on sale, as do other working proofs.

Mangle. Old cast-iron mangles can be modified and used as relief presses.

Manière criblée. See Dotted print.

Manière noire. Where the tonal design is created by rubbing, dissolving or scraping away a solid black field on a mezzotint or aquatint plate or a lithographic matrix.

Margin. The unprinted border around an image.

Masking. The use of various materials, such as liquids, crayons, wax, film, paper, rice grains, sand, etc., which can be used to impede the application of etches or light during the preparation of a printing matrix.

Masonite®. See Hardboard.

Master printer. A skilled printmaking specialist who usually works in collaboration with an artist.

Miss Elizabeth Brownlowe by John Smith, 1685, mezzotint. A typical example of an early mezzotint portrait in 'the English Manner' showing the wide range of tones. © The British Museum/Heritage-Images.

Seed Dispersal by Ione Parkin, 2003. Monotype, 229 x 203 mm (9 x 8 in). Printed and published by the artist.

Master proof. See *Bon à tirer*.

Mat. A US term for a print window mount.

Mat burn. Discoloration of the margins of a print due to the chemical content of an unsuitable, acidic mounting board.

Matrix. The printing surface, which may be stone, metal, wood, linoleum, rubber, plastic, card, board, paper, glass or a stretched screen mesh. It is also the mould from which metal type is cast.

Matt. Usual UK spelling for a mount; also, a dull finish on an ink or paper surface or frame moulding.

Mechanical screen. See Halftone.

Medium. The paper size 458 x 635 mm (18 x 25 in). In printmaking it indicates the specific technique used: relief, intaglio, lithography, screenprinting or digital printmaking. The medium is also the substance or vehicle which binds pigments in ink or paint.

Medium-density fibreboard. MDF is made for the furniture trade but is used for relief blocks.

Mesh. A general term for the woven textile that is stretched over a frame in screenprinting.

Mezzotint. *Manière noire* (French), *Schabmanier* (German), *mezzotinto* (Italian). An engraving technique invented around 1640. A metal plate is indented by rocking a toothed steel tool all over the surface; each pit made will carry ink. The indentations are gradually burnished to reduce their ink-holding depth, thereby creating an infinite variety of tones, from solid black (not burnished) to pure white (highly polished).

Mixed-media print. A print in which several different printing methods are used.

Monochrome print. A single-colour print, sometimes but not always black.

Monoprint. An impression that is different from other prints taken from the same matrix by reason of its colour, paper or finish; a unique print.

Monotype. A unique print whereby the image has to be recreated each time; there is no reusable matrix.

Mordant. A corrosive acid or salt used in etching.

Mould-made paper. See p76.

Mount. See Mat.

Multi-block printing. Where separate blocks or plates are used for each colour but printed together. They may be jigsaw-cut or free-form shapes.

Multi-coloured inking. Where several colours are applied to one block or plate.

Multiple. A mass-produced artwork, often 3D, very popular in the late 1960s.

Multiple edition. More than one edition of the same print, see p102.

Multiple-plate printing. Similar to multi-block printing, but the blocks or plates are all the same size and printed in sequence.

Museum board. An archive-quality mounting board.

Needle. A tool with a steel needlepoint, used in etching to draw the design through the ground thus exposing the metal beneath to acid. Hence 'needling'.

Negative. The result of exposing glass or film coated with a light-sensitive emulsion. The silver salts darken in proportion to the intensity of the light and its duration. A positive can be made from the negative. The term also refers to indirect working (i.e. lift techniques in intaglio), and also to a design with white lines on a black background.

Newsprint. Cheap all-purpose wood-pulp paper used widely in the workshop for initial proofing, and for blotting and mopping up ink.

Numbering. All prints in an edition are numbered in pencil under the image on the left; the first or top number indicates the print number and the second or lower number gives the complete number of prints in the edition, e.g. 51/75.

Number of blocks, etc. The number of printing matrices may not be an accurate record of the number of colours printed, especially when multicoloured inking is used.

Objet trouvé. French for a 'found object', which, if flattish, can be inked and printed. Organic material such as leaves or thin pieces of wood, or fabricated materials such as textiles, string, pressed metal and plastics can all be used either to create a collagraph plate or for impressing into a soft ground on an intaglio plate. Inked impressions can be transferred manually or photographically for lithography, screen and digital work.

Offset. Short for 'offset lithography', whereby the inked image is first picked up by a rubber cylinder and then transferred onto the paper. A relief proof can be offset onto a new block as a cutting guide.

Oleograph. Colour lithograph simulating an oil painting by either bonding the paper print to a canvas backing or embossing the print with a canvas texture; the surface is coated with a varnish and, in the more expensive oleographs, handmade brush strokes completed the deception.

Open bite. Where wide shallow areas of the plate are bitten. The characteristic effect shows some printing ink clinging to the sides, but the bottom is wiped clean.

Original print. See p13.

Overinking. Where too much ink or ink of the wrong viscosity has resulted in the filling-in of the image or a printed squash effect being visible.

Overprinting. Where one colour is printed over another; transparent colours will make a third colour, while opaque colours will cover those beneath.

Paper. A matted sheet of plant or synthetic fibres made by hand or machine.

Paper clay. A mixture of approx. 33 per-cent paper pulp and 67 per-cent clay slip, which can be printed, moulded and fired.

Paper surface. Papers made for artists are supplied in three usual surfaces: HP, hot-pressed, glazed and very smooth; NOT, cold-pressed and with the natural surface left by the couching felt; ROUGH, textured and coarse from couching the sheet on a rough felt.

Paper weight. The old system measured the weight of paper by the ream (500 sheets) regardless of the size of the sheet. Today the measurement is metric and expressed as grams per square metre, gsm or gm2.

Papier Vélin. French for 'wove paper'; not to be confused with *Papier vélin* (lower-case 'v'), which is the French term for 'vellum'.

Papier vergé. French for 'laid paper'.

Papyrus. A proto-paper made from Egyptian reeds which are flattened, cut into strips and laid at right angles with glue. They are then beaten to amalgamate the fibres. Papyrus is still made today.

Parchment. Goat- or sheepskin which can be printed by intaglio or relief. So-called parchment paper is an imitation.

Passed for press. The proof which will serve as the

standard for an edition is signed by the artist to show that the edition can now be printed.

Peau de crapaud. French for 'skin of a toad', which describes the texture of fine reticulated lithographic washes.

pH scale. A logarithmic scale for expressing acidity and alkalinity. Neutral is pH7; below that is acidic, and above is alkaline.

Photomechanical. A broad term for any reproductive process which uses photography to create the printing matrix.

Photopolymers. A group of plastics which are light-sensitive. Used in the form of emulsion and film, which are applied to a backing of metal, board or screen and then exposed and developed. Pre-coated plates for intaglio and relief are also obtainable.

Photosensitive. A film or liquid which reacts to light and produces a chemical change in the form of hardening, as in photographic film and paper. Hence 'photo-etching', 'photolitho' and 'photoscreen'.

Pinxit. Latin for 'painted this', as seen on old prints.

Pirated copy. Infringement of copyright.

Pixels. The tiny dots which make up the image on a computer screen and a computer-printed image.

Planographic. Printing from a flat surface, such as in lithography and some forms of monotype. The term has also been used to include screenprinting, but today that is considered a separate medium in its own right.

Plaster print. A print taken from an engraved plaster-of-Paris block. A print can also be taken from an inked intaglio plate by making a temporary retaining wall round the plate and pouring on plaster. When it has set the plate is removed to show a perfect image in plaster.

Plate-mark. The edge of a plate indented in the paper, the sign of an intaglio print. False plate-marks are sometimes seen on reproductions.

Pochoir. French for 'hand-stencilling'. It was once a common way of adding colour to book illustrations and posters, and has been revived recently by artists.

Posterisation. A colour image is scanned using the four standard filters for CMYK; in addition each colour receives three exposures: light, medium and dark. When an image is printed in 12 colours (often a modification of CMYK) the effect appears much richer

Scrubland by Ione Parkin, 2002. Solar etching (photopolymer), 228 x 178 mm (9 x 7 in). Printed and published by the artist.

than the usual 4-colour reproduction. It was widely used on screen prints during the 1970s.

Press. A mechanical device for exerting pressure on a printing matrix for transferring ink to paper. Hand-operated or mechanised; direct or indirect (offset); flatbed, rotary, cylinder, platen, hydraulic or for screen-printing.

Pressure. The force required to print by hand or mechanical means.

Pressure gap. The space in a picture frame between any glazing and the print.

Print. The image on the paper or other substrate is usually described according the medium used to make it, e.g. an etching, an aquatint, a screenprint.

Print book. Records of each edition should be kept by the artist.

Print cabinet. *Cabinet des estampes* (French),

Druckekabinett (German), *calcografía* (Spanish/Italian). A print collection in a museum.

Printer. The person operating a press or taking the print impression – it may be the artist or a collaborator or technician. Obviously, 'printer' also refers to the computer attachment for outputting stored information.

Printer's proof. One of the copies extra to the edition, kept for the printer's archive.

Printing order. The order of printing the colours must take into account the effect each colour will have on the others.

Print on demand. The printing of individual copies as required is now common in digital printing.

Private press. In 1933, Eric Gill defined a private press as 'one that prints solely what it chooses to print'.

Process engraving. Photomechanical halftone blocks in one-, three- or four-colour systems for commercial letterpress printing.

Progressive proofs. Colour proofs which are taken to check registration and order. The sequence shows each colour separately and then colour one plus two; one, two plus three; and so on. See p66.

Proof. A trial print, hence 'proofing'.

Provenance. The history of the ownership of a work of art.

Publisher. The person who issues and sells prints and artist's books.

Publisher's proof. A copy of the print or book for the publisher's records.

Pull. An impression taken at any stage before editioning.

Pulp. A mixture of water and plant fibres from which paper is made.

Reduction print. A print using only one printing matrix for a multicoloured image; it can be relief, screen or lithographic. The entire edition is printed in the first colour. Parts of the image are then removed and the second colour is printed, and so on until all the colours are printed. Also called a 'suicide' or 'elimination' print.

Register marks. These can be seen on some proofs in the form of two crosses at either end on the short sides of the paper, either printed or cut out; they may also appear as dots or pinholes. Once the registration

French Landscape by Rosemary Simmons HonRE, 1957. Lift-ground aquatint, printed relief (surface-inked) and intaglio showing a negative and positive image.

of all colours is satisfactory the crosses and dots can be removed, and thus will not be seen on edition copies.

Registration. The correct positioning of one colour with another. Depending on the method of printing, many different register plans can be used: lay marks, register marks, Kento, pins, needles, T-bar, notches, studs, paper clamping or nipping under the cylinder in an intaglio press, or the naked eye.

Relief etching. A surface-printed intaglio plate. See p64.

Relief printing. Printing from just the surface of a block or plate. Examples are woodcut, wood engraving, linocut, letterpress, relief etching, etc.

Reproduction. The duplication of a pre-existing painting or drawing by photomechanical or digital processes or by a copyist, i.e. not an artist's original print.

Reprographics. A general word covering printing, copying and the preparatory work for commercial printing.

Repoussage. French for the technique of hammering on the back of a metal plate on a burnished area to raise the surface again.

Restrike. The reprinting of a plate, block or stone. Certain printers still keep a stock of popular images that they print to order. These are usually old topographical or hunting scenes; they are not signed or numbered. They may be of historical interest but are not in the same category as artist's original prints.

Retroussage. Ink is dragged out of parts or all of an intaglio plate using a soft cloth, giving a richer tone.

Reversal of the image. The image on the printing matrix must be in reverse in relief, intaglio and direct lithography. The image does not have to be reversed in offset lithography and screenprinting.

Rice paper. A generalised term for any Asian paper, though it is not made from rice. However, there is a fragile culinary 'paper', made from dried rice paste, which can be used for edible prints.

Rice paste. Used for paper sizing, paper gluing and as an additive to bind water-based printing colours.

Rocker. A toothed steel tool which is rocked back and forth over a metal plate to create a mezzotint plate textured with ink-holding pits.

Roller. Used to distribute ink evenly on a printing matrix.

Roulette. A steel engraving tool with a small spiked wheel which makes a dotted texture on an intaglio plate. It is often used where an aquatint has been rubbed down and some ink-holding pits need to be re-incised.

Royal. A paper size, approx. 510 x 675 mm (20 x 25 in).

Rubber stamp. Small relief blocks cut into rubber (pencil rubbers can be used), or they can be photo-graphically produced from polymers. Rubber stamps can be printed on delicate surfaces such as ceramic.

Rubbing. See *Frottage.*

Safe printmaking. A movement started in the 1980s as a result of new health-and-safety laws to replace the more noxious and carcinogenic materials habitually used by printmakers. Also called 'non-toxic printmaking'.

Salt aquatint. Household salt is sprinkled on an intaglio plate with a not-quite-dry hard ground. When the plate is heated the salt drops through the ground onto the metal. The ground is allowed to solidify, and when the plate is placed in water the salt dissolves, leaving a random, open texture similar to an aquatint.

Sandpaper. Used for various abrasive purposes, but an intact sheet can be impressed into a soft ground giving an aquatint-like texture. If it is placed on a copper sheet and placed under the pressure of an intaglio press, the result is similar but not as good as a rocked mezzotint plate.

Screen. A rectangular frame of wood or metal over which a woven mesh of silk, synthetic textile or metal wire is stretched. In screenprinting, this supports a stencil. See also Halftone.

Screen filler. A thick liquid used to fill the holes between mesh threads in the non-printing areas of a stencil.

Screen painting. An image can be painted with soluble ink, paint or crayon on the outside of a screen. When dry, it is printed using a base suitable to dissolve the image-making material; the result is a monotype.

Screenprint. A stencil print made using a mesh-covered frame or screen which supports a stencil.

Sculpsit. Latin for 'engraved this', as seen on old prints.

Second editions. When an uncancelled matrix is reprinted. Not to be encouraged.

Serigraph. A name given to artist-printed screenprints as opposed to commercial screenprinting. The term is still used in the USA and Europe.

Serigraphy. The term was devised from the early use of silk as mesh material for screen-printing.

Sieve print. An early name for a 'screenprint'.

Signature. The artist's signature in pencil conveys approval.

Signed on the plate. A printed signature, which implies that not every print has been individually approved by the artist, if any.

Siligraphy. A term used for an artist's print using waterless lithography.

Stirring by Jane Stobart RE. Soft-ground etching, 270 x 157 mm (10 ⅝ x 6⅛ in)

Silk aquatint. A form of collagraph using a textile mesh glued to a backing board. Non-printing areas are blocked out with acrylic paint mixed with acrylic medium or gel; these smooth areas can be wiped clean, but ink is held in the pockets between the threads of the mesh.

Silk screen. Another name for a 'screenprint', even though silk is rarely used today.

Size. A print has two sizes, one denoting the image size and one the paper size; height is traditionally given first. Size (animal or cellulose glue) is also used strengthen paper.

Soft ground. Grease is added to intaglio hard ground to make it soft and receptive to marks or objects pressed into it, which then lift off the ground and allow acid to bite the metal exposed. This can be done by drawing on the back of a sheet of thin paper laid over the soft-grounded plate or by laying things like leaves or feathers on the plate and running it through the press.

Solander box. A storage box for works on paper.

Solar print. The Australian name for photopolymer etching (flexography) using the sun as a light source.

Spirit ground. An alternative to dusting resin for aquatint. Resin particles are suspended in alcohol, and the ground is poured over an intaglio plate. The alcohol evaporates, leaving the particles in a random pattern.

Spit biting. Used to etch small areas of a plate. Spit is applied using a feather and acid dropped onto the plate; the acid will not spread. Gum can be used instead of spit.

Spray ground. An intaglio ground applied from a spray.

Squeegee. A rubber or urethane blade, held in a wooden or metal frame, used to push ink through a screen.

Stamp. To impress an inked or uninked block onto a substrate. An embossing stamp has two parts, male and female, which clamp the paper between the dies.

States. State proofs are taken each time a print has been added to or had something taken away, so that the progress of the work can be checked.

Steel engraving. An engraving on steel, which can be printed in very large numbers with little wear; characterised by a hard, precise line.

Steel-facing. The electroplating of intaglio plates to make them suitable for printing large editions without wear. Also applied to copperplates when red, yellow and some other inks are used which might discolour in contact with copper.

Stencil. See *Pochoir* and Screenprinting.

Stenocut. A relief-printing material made from commercial rubber, it is easy to cut and prints well.

Stipple. Fine dots drawn to give an impression of a tone. Stipple engraving was an 18th-century engraving technique using the point of a graver.

Stochastic. A mathematical formula for producing random halftone dot patterns.

Stone. Solnhofen stone from Bavaria is considered the best lithographic stone, though many others have been used, such as marble, slate, white lias and soapstone. Abrasive stones are used for sharpening tools and to erase lithographic work.

Stopping out. An acid resist used in etching to stop some areas from any further etching; varnish, wax and acrylic liquids are used.

Substrate. The sheet that is printed; usually paper but it can be card, plastic, metal, textile, leather, clay or wood.

Sugar lift. An intaglio technique using a solution of sugar, water and some colouring to make it visible, which is painted on a metal plate. Once dry it is covered by a liquid ground; when that is dry the plate is immersed in water, which dissolves the sugar thus lifting off the drawing. The plate is normally given an aquatint ground, either before or after the liquid ground is applied, so as to hold the ink.

Surface tone. A slight film of ink is left on an intaglio plate after cleaning, giving the print an overall tint or tone.

Title page. The page at the beginning of a book or portfolio of prints which gives the title, artist and/or author, publisher and date. The other details, such as edition size and printer, medium and materials, are usually given on a separate sheet or page called the 'imprint' or 'colophon'.

Tradigital. A term used for a print which uses both traditional and digital printmaking methods.

Transfer paper. A gum-arabic coated paper is used by artists to draw an image away from the print studio. It is later transferred to the printing stone or plate. See also Laser-transfer paper.

Trial proof. A proof to test registration, colour, paper and position.

Trimming. The cutting down of the margins of a print, usually to fit a frame, is not good practice. The margins around an image are carefully chosen by the artist and are part of the whole print.

Tusche. Derived from the German word for 'Indian ink'. A liquid-ink emulsion for lithographic drawing, with a suitable grease content.

Ultraviolet light. Electromagnetic light which hardens

Clearing up by Jane Stobart RE. Sugar lift etching, 270 × 157 mm (10 ⅝ × 6 ⅛ in).

most photographic and photopolymer compounds.

Undercutting. If an image on a block or plate is undercut at the edges of the work, the material may break down under pressure. The term is also used when light creeps under a negative or positive because contact is bad during exposure.

Unique impression. A single print which is not repeatable in that particular form. It could also be a trial proof, an abandoned image, a monoprint or a monotype.

Unlimited or unrestricted edition. An edition which is not signed or numbered and does not have a stated total print run. See p36.

Tower of Babel by Anne Desmet RE, 2002. Relief print from wooden type, wood engraving, linocut, flexograph with collage. This is a unique print.

Unpublished plate. A printing matrix as yet unpublished; usually found after an artist's death, whereupon it may be posthumously published.

Vacuum bed. A screenprinting table with a vacuum base which holds the printing paper flat during printing. Exposure units may also have a vacuum bed to ensure close contact of the negative or positive with the coated matrix.

Varnish. A clear sticky substance used as a vehicle in inks and also to adhere metallic foils and powders.

Vatman. The handmade-paper craftsman who lifts the paper pulp from the vat using a mould and deckle. After preliminary draining, he hands it to the coucher, who turns the sheet of paper onto a felt; another felt is then placed on top ready for the next sheet.

Vehicle. The base liquid which carries pigment: water in watercolours, gouache and drawing ink; varnish, oils, acrylics or cellulose for a variety of printing inks.

Viscosity. The relative fluidity of printing inks.

Viscosity intaglio printing. A method of applying several coloured inks in layers on one printing plate for multicoloured printing. It is based on the principle that inks of different viscosities will not mix.

Wallpaper-paste ink. Cheap screen-printing ink made from cellulose paste and dyes or pigments.

Waste sheets. Sheets of paper used during proofing; they are often recycled many times in workshops.

Watercolour. Finely ground pigments bound by glue and dissolved in water.

Waterleaf paper. Unsized paper; it is very absorbent and weak when dampened, but very suitable for relief, lithography and screen-printing.

Waterless lithography. A recent development in lithography whereby the water-attracting non-image areas are replaced by an ink-rejecting surface made from a silicone compound. As water is not used, commercial presses can run faster and paper is not affected by dampness. Artists have devised a system suitable for the smaller print workshop.

The intaglio workshop at Spike Island Printmakers, Bristol, UK. A community class of disabled people, the Artists First Group, is in progress. Several intaglio presses can be seen in the background.

Watermark. A design seen in a sheet of paper when held up to the light. It can be important in identifying the origin of the paper.

Wax. Used as an acid and alkali resist and added to some drawing materials.

White ground. A form of lift ground using soap powder, titanium white pigment, linseed oil and water. See Lift ground.

White-line engraving. A characteristic of wood engraving whereby the design appears printed as white lines on a dark background.

Woodblock print. The Western term for a traditional Chinese or Japanese woodcut print using water-based colours.

Woodcut. A print taken from a block of wood cut lengthways with the grain.

Wood engraving. A print taken from a block of wood cut through the end grain. Sometimes the term is used by historians for a woodcut in which fine engraving tools have been used instead of the coarser woodcutting tools.

Wood-free paper. No mechanical wood pulp is added to the paper. Mechanical wood pulp is made by grinding up wood and contains lignin, which yellows the paper. Chemical wood pulp is made by extracting the lignin, leaving pure cellulose fibres from which good-quality papers can be wholly or partly made.

Wood pulp. It was first used to make paper in 1800 and since around 1850 has been the material used in most commercial paper manufacture.

Workshop. A printmaker's studio, which ideally is well-lit and well-ventilated, with a sound floor to bear the weight of a heavy printing press and with adequate space for all activities. Printmakers often share workshops on a cooperative basis; other workshops are set up for professional editioning.

Wove paper. A papermaker's mould using fine woven wire was introduced in 1757. It gave a much smoother paper without visible laid lines.

Xerography. A trade name for a form of electrostatic printing commonly used by office copiers. Although it is used by artists, it is not acceptable for quality artist's prints.

Xylography. Derived from the Greek for 'wood', hence its use to describe wood engraving and woodcutting.

Zinc. Metal sheet used for intaglio and lithographic plates.

Zincography. An obsolete term for lithography produced from grained zinc plates.

Index